| PRAISE FOR *The Light Inside the Dark*

"An exquisite book which welcomes you in its arms and carries your deepest longings and loves with the lyrical voice of a nightingale. This is one of the best guides yet to the breaking open of the human heart, to vulnerability, eternal spirit, and the mountains dancing."

—JACK KORNFIELD, AUTHOR OF *A Path with Heart*

"John Tarrant offers us a way to gain access to the irrepressible seeds of hope which lie barren, yet ready to bloom, in fallow, and dark times. He does this by stretching the imagination of the Western mind to include—for soul's sake—not only its own stories of Greek gods and goddesses, the great fathers of the Hebrew Bible, and the redemption possible in Jesus' life, but also the great teachings of Zen Buddhist masters and the best spiritual exercises of the East."

—CLARISSA PINKOLA ESTÉS, PH.D., AUTHOR OF *Women Who Run With the Wolves, The Gift of Story,* AND *The Faithful Gardener*

"This book invites superlatives. It is an exquisite mapping of the Buddhist and totally beyond Buddhist path of liberation, done with the lightest of touches, with perfect grace and clarity and warmth of heart, in a way that makes it so human, and so compelling, that it shows this path, and the work/play of meditation, to be nothing less than life itself, the human condition, offering anyone and everyone the actualities, the shadows, the blossoms, and the boundless, ever-present possibilities of a life lived in awareness, with nothing holding."

—JON KABAT-ZINN, AUTHOR OF *Wherever You Go, There You Are*; COAUTHOR OF *Everyday Blessings: The Inner Work of Mindful Parenting*

"John Tarrant's subject is the unbearable lightness of being but also its inconsolable heaviness, and his thinking about the relation between these two poles of spirit and soul is extraordinarily rich. He inoculates one against the wish for a quick fix in the spiritual or imaginative life. His work is useful to poets in the way Bachelard's *Poetics of Space* or Hyde's *The Gift* is useful."

—ROBERT HASS, FORMER POET LAUREATE OF THE UNITED STATES

"To accept Tarrant's invitation to search for 'the light inside the dark' is to become swept up in a torrent of evocative and lyrical images which move seamlessly from the mythology of ancient Greece through the humorous asceticism of Zen masters to the passionate pain of modern psychotherapeutic patients."

—*Publishers Weekly*

The Light Inside the Dark

Zen, Soul, and the Spiritual Life

John Tarrant

Foreword by
Stephen Mitchell

HarperPerennial
A Division of HarperCollinsPublishers

Designed and typeset by David Bullen Design

The Library of Congress has catalogued the hardcover edition as follows:
Tarrant, John, 1949–
The light inside the dark : Zen, soul and the spiritual life / John Tarrant. — 1st ed.
p.   cm.
ISBN 0–06–017219–3
1. Spiritual life   2. Spiritual life—Zen buddhism—Miscellanea.   I. Title
BL624.T37   1998
291.4—dc21   98–17676

ISBN 0-06-093111-6 (pbk.)

99 00 01 02 03 ❖/RRD 10 9 8 7 6 5 4 3 2 1

For Sarah

Contents

Acknowledgments

This book has been a ten years' work. During that time I dreamed it was a large fish, a transpacific yacht, a fishing boat, and a hot-rodded destroyer. Fish just appear, or don't appear I suppose, and are independent of us, but to the extent that this book is a vessel and a made thing, it has been built by many hands—the ideas, labor, and love of many friends.

Stephen Mitchell, my old Dharma brother, supported the work from the beginning with friendship, advice, and money.

Michael Katz once told me that, being too lazy to write his own books, he tries to get his friends to write them for him. Along with Stephen, he suggested I write this one and has been a good friend.

Hugh Van Dusen has been most gracious and helpful.

Two first-rate writers have touched each page:

Jane Hirshfield's magisterial editing gave the book coherence, shape, and encouragement.

Noelle Oxenhandler was the psychopomp of the book: writing coach, guide through its underworld, opener of closed doors.

Many helped in other ways:

Robert Aitken with his teacher, Koun Yamada, brought the old, high teachings of Zen and koans to the West and worked life-long to share them. Jack Kornfield has been mixing western and eastern ideas about consciousness for a long time. Sylvia Boorstein offered her thoughts on compassion. Joan Sutherland's imaginative Zen teaching has provided a laboratory for the ideas on enlightenment expressed here and she's been a good friend as well. Other Zen teachers—Subhana Barzaghi, Ross Bolleter, Daniel Terragno, David Weinstein, Susan Murphy, James Ford, and Jonathan Joseph—are also closely involved in this practicum. Roberta Goldfarb is mixing Zen and Vipassana and ideas of the relatedness of psyche, and supported the book with her friendship from the first. Lamas Yeshe and Zopa first taught me the Tibetan meditations mentioned. René Tillich's ideas of demons and their value in the psyche are here. Rachel Remen shared her thoughts on healing and lent me her house to write in. Mayumi Oda's passion for the creative and Nancy Colvin's thoughts on love and service are here too.

Others whose voices have entered the book in some way, large or small, include James Anthony, Edgar Auerswald, Lynn Bouguereau, David Bubna-Litic, Patti Burke, Tyrone Cashman, Dana Dantine, Trish Dougherty, Julian Gresser, Michael Kieran, Neil

Russack, Michael Sierchio, Lyn Silbert, Joan Smith, Maureen Sweeney.

The writings of C. G. Jung and James Hillman are a starting point for consideration of soul and spirit. The writings of Hakuin Ekaku provide a Zen model for interest in soul. Some organizations have given me a home for the work I do: these include the California Diamond Sangha Zen Centers in Santa Rosa, Oakland, Fresno, and Palo Alto; the Sydney and Perth Zen Centres in Australia; VNA & Home Hospice of Santa Rosa; and the Program in Integrative Medicine at the University of Arizona in Tucson. Those who have worked with me in Zen and in psychotherapy have been generous in allowing me to share their discoveries.

Foreword

It is obvious from its first pages, its first sentences, that *The Light Inside the Dark* is a profoundly original and important book. You can feel the quality of John Tarrant's thinking in his finely wrought verbal intelligence, which is skeptical of abstractions and works close to the bone. With a prose rich in the things of this world, and an insight honed by twenty-five years of intensive Zen training, Tarrant has created not so much a synthesis as a brilliant reimagining of the great inner traditions of East and West. He maps the landscape of the inner life and takes us on a journey through it, so that we can feel its terrain under our feet, gaze into its abysses, and lie down under its stars.

This is a beautiful, passionate, meticulously forthright book. It is not merely acquainted with the night but intimate with it, modest yet rooted in essential wisdom, personal yet informed by the strength of what is beyond personality. The usual categories of psychology seem irrelevant here. At this depth, psychology itself is the reverse side of theology, and mysticism is as matter-of-fact as the glass of orange juice on your breakfast table. Here originality is largely a question of returning to origins: knowing the place we all begin from.

Tarrant is not the first writer to distinguish between *soul* and *spirit,* two words that are vaguely synonymous both in the ancient languages and in ordinary usage. But he has broadened and clarified this distinction, and in doing so he has given us new words. Even more important, at a time when it is fashionable to favor soul over spirit, he has treated both sides of the dichotomy with his respectful attention, "an attention so persevering that it becomes a kind of love." This impartiality allows him to penetrate deeply into the split that any dichotomy creates. We crave not only what the soul craves—depth, darkness, embodiment, the poetry and turmoil of this world, any element that allows us to suffer and mature; but also the cravings of the spirit—for light, purity, birth-and-death-lessness, the dazzle of true insight, the unshakable knowledge of our primal identity. We can't go deep unless we are willing to go high, since the way up and the way down are one and the same.

Nor can we speak of spirit and soul in a fruitful way if we take the words too seriously. Ultimately, they are just a manner of speaking, as Tarrant knows very well. One of the delicious ironies of his book is that he is a teacher of Buddhism, which begins from the fundamental perception that there is no such thing as soul or spirit or self. No such thing? But this no-thing beams at us and demands our attention, like the "grin without a cat" that beams at Alice from another giver of non-directions.

The journey that Tarrant takes us on leads to enlightenment and beyond enlightenment. On this journey, going means letting go. It's not all that hard to get enlightened; what is difficult is to keep giving up our sense of the world so that the world can come to us on its own terms, with its vast, pitiless, loving intelligence. At the end of the journey, we return to the simplest things with an immense recognition and gratitude, a recognition and gratitude that I hope you will feel as you arrive at the last pages of this book.

STEPHEN MITCHELL

The Light Inside the Dark

Chapter 1

Invitation to the Journey

The Inward Voyage

How lovely!
Through the torn paper screen,
the Milky Way.

ISSA

When we were children our days were full of wonder—the world unfolded itself and ourselves at the same time. In such an eternal afternoon the grass hums, the ball flies into the blue, and the girl sings the skipping-rope song:

Cindereller dressed in yeller
went upstairs to kiss a feller;
made a mistake and kissed a snake.
How many doctors did it take?

imagining the time when she will be bitten by a life that is still being dreamed and has not yet arrived—though it is clear to her father, watching, that life is here for her now, utterly complete.

Beneath or inside the life we lead every day is another life. This unseen life runs like a river beneath the city, beneath work, family, ambition, beneath our pleasures and griefs. "There is another world," says Paul Eluard, "and it is inside this one."

In the helter-skelter, in the rush to get an education, to make a career, to make a family, to find material success, to hurry, to do, to survive, this interior life is often subjugated or paved over. The life that in the child is something vivid and whole goes further inward in the adult, where it usually slumbers until it is called forth. But this life beneath or within our ordinary life is irrepressible, unstoppable: it comes up in loveliness like jonquils out of fallen snow, it rises in supplication like hands out of gratings in a pavement in India, and it bursts upward through our chests as the fountain of shock that is our reaction to evil news. It appears in dreams, revery, memories of childhood, in what we find beautiful, and in what we find ugly as a gargoyle, and appears too when we fall in love, when we fall ill, when we are lost on dark paths. It touches our pleasures with melancholy and intermittently pierces our desperation with joy.

I have always loved to think of the old navigators—the small bands moving to a new continent over land bridges made by the ice age; the Polynesian canoe masters, sailing into the vastness with a coconut shell half filled with water, observation holes drilled into it near the rim; James Cook, who rose through the ranks to command the ship *Endeavour*, carrying Joseph Banks to botanize through these same Pacific islands; and my own ancestors, transported in chains to the desolation of Botany Bay.

Whether or not our travels may eventually extend to the stars and those brave, hard-pressed voyages be repeated in some new form, our frontier now is the inner life. In this book, two great lineages of inward exploration are brought together. The first is the Asian tradition with its long devotion to the arts of attention and to a spiritual understanding based on inquiry and experience rather than dogma. The second is the Western method of work with the soul, with exploring the life of feeling, thought, and the stories and legends that the soul likes to tell, stories in which we trace our destiny through pain and joy, to find out what happens next.

The inward voyage and the outer both have an heroic aspect. Outer voyages make new connections by which human beings achieve many ends—adventure, trade, conquest, and love. The inner voyage also makes new connections: it plunges us into an initiatory space, the way young boys were once thrust into the forecastle of a sailing ship; then, as the world we have known disappears, we are rocked and whirled around until the ship anchors once more in a harbor. We step ashore in a land that is not externally new but that our eyes, being changed, see in its primeval freshness. The interior voyage overcomes loneliness by offering us a place in the universe, where we can know ourselves in the midst of all changes.

If we respect the inner life, we find that it is also possible to reverse the whole relationship between inner and outer, beneath and above, and make the inner life come first, as a garden that is tended for the tending's own sake. To cultivate, to know, to love this vast inscape is the only way to be free in any circumstances, the only way to mend the poverty of wasted years. We explore the interior realm because it is what we humans are for—consciousness, the marvelous voyage.

Much of the journey is about the ways we work with our attention, because attention gives us more life. It expands the register, bringing us to notice more of the vividness and consolation of our dark lives, so that we can exist in our true range, and not go around missing things, as if we knew countries only from their airports and hotels. Attention is the most basic form of love: through it we bless and are blessed. When we attend to the interior life, we also connect with what surrounds us—the espresso machine hissing, the skipping rope with its two red handles in line and the rope curling lazily out and back, the green points on the snowdrops nodding over the cold ground. What was matter and merely inanimate becomes family, and we, the children walking, walking, walking home. All wanting—for love, to be seen for who we are, for a new red car—is wanting to find and be taken into this mysterious depth in things. And it is this inner connection that resolves the problem of who we are and makes us at home in the world. For the interior life sweetens the humblest thing. It opens for us the magic in ordinary life.

The Method of the Book

Some books are maps that tell you where you can go. This book attempts instead to give you some of the taste, excitement, and sense of being subjected to extremes that are typical of the interior journey. The method of the book is to connect things that are usually far apart, allowing them their natural difference and tension, and so to arrive at balance by amplitude rather than by fasting. It tries to give the feel of the voyage the way a novel does, transforming the journey through our dangerous, beautiful life by bringing an ever-deepening attention to it.

There is blood as well as happiness in these pages. We look into the darkest moments—death, loss, and ignorance—in order to find evidence for the presence of the spirit and the soul. For if the spirit is real, and if the soul is real, they must console us in the thickest night, they must be found precisely *there*, where they seem most absent. In my life as a teacher of Zen and as a psychotherapist, people have told me their stories, holding nothing back. Using those tales, so generously given, I have mapped out the journey. From the first, I found that I could not stand at a distance from the material either: when night came over the journey, I would myself grow dark and fragmented, and when the journey turned upwards to brightness, I too would become enlightened in that moment.

I hope you will recognize your own life here as well, and that you will find yourself in conversation with the many voices in the book. I imagine too that the voices of your own journey will appear in you, reciting the ways they are similar to and the ways they are different from the voices I have recorded here. In the middle of such a chorus, we can sometimes see the way the personal is nested within a relentless, universal process. And we can see also how once we give ourselves over to it fully, we are borne up by the journey itself. Sometimes this book asks you to jump from voice to voice and from image to image, mirroring the imaginative act that life itself asks of us, when, pressing us hard, it reveals an underlying order, the more authentic because composed of broken, disparate pieces.

There is the voice of the shaman calling the ancestors into the community of the living; the voice of the initiating elder bringing purifying ordeals; the voice of the Buddhist meditator whose laboratory is the interior life; the voice of the dreamer heading into the labyrinth and the voice of the psychotherapist holding the other end of the thread of that dream; the voice of the nineteenth-century essayist who quotes classics on mundane occasions in order to honor them; the voice of the lover; the voice of the mother who has lost her child; the voice of the man dying of AIDS; the voice of the executive making a deal; the voice of the ordinary person whose only desire is to flow smoothly through life; the voice of the scientist asking "What really happens?" and the voice of the child asking "What comes next?"

Voices of pain and voices of delight, dark material and bright— all are useful for the journey. At the same time there is a central core: each voice sings its note of eternity. There are spirit books that talk about spirit and soul books that talk about soul—in this book I have tried to hold these two great archetypes in conversation with each other, letting them murmur tenderly to each other and groan in pain, letting them shout out in joy for what is found and wail for what is lost and cannot be recovered. Underlying all the voices I hope you will hear a unifying consciousness, telling the old story of going out and coming home, as if by firelight in a cave, so that the children listening now with upturned faces will know, when their turn comes, that others have gone before and that they are not alone.

Chapter 2

The Wildness Inside and the Creatures to Be Found There

Into the Primeval Place

The interior life is a place of the wild—uncivilized and unpredictable, giving us fevers, symptoms, and moments of impossible beauty. Yet within the appearances of chaos are both a richness and a deep level of orderliness. Like a national park, the interior world doesn't *do* anything—it is the treasure-house of life. It can't be strip-mined for our conscious purposes. The only request it makes of us is that we love it, and, in return, it responds to our attention. To learn to attend well is to discover our place in the natural order: it brings an element of consistency and harmony to our lives and gives us a story about who we are. To learn to attend is a beginning. To learn to attend more and more deeply is the path itself.

For aboriginal people, a wilderness is not something alien but a kind of blessed garden. As our attention deepens, we too come to harmonize with existence, learn to see the thin vine that has a tuber underneath or to follow the direction of the birds at sunset to a waterhole. Gradually we change. Our listening becomes more acute, we hear background as well as foreground noises, and we are no longer so surprised by the animals—the fears and longings of our inner life—and do not complain that someone else has caused their rough ways. When our attention is offered freely, the inner life in return becomes a friend to comfort and sustain us. Gradually, through our offered attention, we connect with the source out of which we came—we become aboriginal to ourselves, discovering how much we love our own inwardness.

The Transparence of Spirit

Sometimes we want to live inside the source itself, and bend toward it like the heliotrope to changing light. To take this path, this whole direction, is to face toward *spirit*. We take up such a way for many reasons—for health, to live in goodness, to answer our great questions—but there is an element of unreason too, for we fall in love with spirit. Spirit is the center of life, the light out of which we are born with eyes still reflecting the vastness, and the light toward which our eyes turn when our breath goes out and does not come in again.

The great inner traditions, from paleolithic shamanism to monastic Christianity, have brought us many disciplines to cultivate our link with spirit. Such work involves meditation, prayer, and the slow, delicious process of letting go—everything we thought important drops away when the blaze and stillness at the center fills the view.

Meditation—the primary method of spiritual inquiry, taking various forms in different traditions—plunges us into the source and saturates us with its waters, answering, in a certain fashion, our curiosity about what it is that we are. When we turn toward spirit, it compels us to its mode, in which eternity is everlastingly present within our lives, making the smallest moment vibrant and full of color. Our underlying doubts about existence soften, and a constricting attachment to the narrow, received aspects of consciousness is weakened. The transparence of the world amazes us—at each moment we are surprised anew by the clarity of what we see: our undeniable connection to the source. We have come home at last, no longer alone on the earth.

Spirit is *given*. It is not produced by our attention, it is uncovered—showing us our link from the beginning with all of life, with frogs and trees and stones. And it is not more fond of us than it is of frogs, trees, and stones. Bearing us past the deepest pains we suffer, past grief, war, and death, it underlies all things.

Spirit's path is real, heroic, and enormously seductive, and its revelation is always the same—in an experience of enlightenment or awakening, the veils that obscure our view are lifted and our oneness with God and the universe is revealed. The wilderness is clearly recognized as a garden, and as our original home. To spirit, morality is a natural thing: like a hill it is just *there*—the good and the bad are clear but unexamined. Similarly, for spirit each moment is a fragment of eternity; *just this* is the ancient treasure of consciousness, and the portion of earth and time we inhabit now is the actuality of the everlasting fire.

Through attentiveness to spirit, we enter a place of reverence, of such a deep witnessing of life that it is a kind of illumination. We see that woman, river, wind, and star are all equal, and that death and life are both dreamlike processes, themselves part of a greater unchangingness. We are impressed by these discoveries, which have a natural dazzle to them; we are happy, we feel we have something that we can rely on. Just to have seen this world as it is seems enough for a lifetime. Even were we to die the same evening, we have seen eternity and it is enough.

The experience of spirit is natural, and most people have had a taste of it. Still, to know its consistent presence in our lives requires a discipline that seems severe at first. This discipline is the daily work of meditation and prayer. A steady practice evokes the feeling and imagery of winter—the cold that works on the bare, naked boughs, preparing them for spring. Then, after we have plodded and endured, there is something arbitrary and astonishing about the irruption of spirit into awareness: nothing prepares us for the sudden grace of the plum blossoms.

And if the spirit's road has its true magic, it also has its dark, unregarded losses. For spirit is only a portion; it does not define either the whole journey or the whole of the republic. In Buddhist thought, spirit might be referred to as the pure body of the Buddha, or else as a realm of vast emptiness, where everything is possible because there is no content. The earth, and our life upon it, are founded on a mystery that is clearly seen, and shines in all directions. This dimension of spirit is the most wonderful thing there is; and yet, alone, it is strangely helpless.

Part of spirit's weakness is that it is so clear about its goals, and so reckless and headlong in their pursuit. Mr. Bugatti, the founder of the automobile company that bore his name, was asked why his racing cars had poor brakes. He replied, "I make them to go, not stop," and this is very like the spirit's point of view—thoroughgoing, full of absolutes.

Adept at transcendence, spirit gives us the foundation for understanding reality, but is of little help with the day-to-day arts of relishing life. As in those Renaissance paintings that show just the feet of Jesus as he disappears out the top of the picture, spirit wants only to ascend, to be pure. Always getting by with less so that it can encompass more, spirit forgets to feed the kids or hold a job. It lacks poetry, melancholy, and everything voluptuous. These it leaves to others, as if it needed servants to do its living for it.

God's Feet

To enter the realm of spirit, then, is only a part of the solution to the dilemma proposed by this found process, life. The remaining art resides in living well, in the particulars of our movement through the day and night. And this means attending to the second impulse of inner life—being interested in the feet of God, the parts that are still visible and have not ascended out of the picture. These toes and calloused skin are the neglected element of the divine, the bit that touches the earth: the bit we have.

This second impulse, simultaneous with and contradictory to the first, takes us toward the little and the disregarded: the valley world that is lovely, seductive, transient, destructive of our illusions and also of our wisdom—not the life eternal, but the life that we die of. Even full of loss, even full of disease, this aspect of existence too is good. It has its point of view and its disciplines. It does not replace but intermingles with the spirit. This lower part is bound on the wheel of time—it loves the sound of rain and the smell of basil, it stands at the foot of the bed feeling the heart enlarge before the face of the sleeping child; it is the servant who tends to life, who tastes and touches life, who *is* life. The lower part is what we offer back to eternity, our contribution, and it makes a way for eternity to live through us. In accordance with the Mediterranean tradition and the current conventions of depth psychology, let us call it *soul*. In this usage, soul is not taken in the theological sense of an immortal being putting up for the night in the inn of the body—that is spirit. Soul is that part of us which touches and is touched by the world. Through soul we connect with each other and are made less lonely—not metaphysically, but in a tangible, human way.

The Soul's Pagan Joy

In love with the multitudinous world, soul is pagan: it falls headlong into matter. Scattering its affections, it likes to merge—with chocolate, gardening, a fast car, a lost love. And while it brings delight, it brings misery too, joining with rage, jealousy, and vanity. Where spirit is certain of its paths, soul, like Dante in the dark wood, is always losing its way. It obsesses and broods: like Proust, it is drawn back and back into a childhood still vivid and full of causes. It is with our souls that we truly inhabit our lives, tasting the fresh black coffee, so delicious, so bad for us, and the kiss, so brief and full of consequences. Soul is always learning, always fallible; it develops well or ill, it grows and deepens and responds to our late-learned tenderness toward it. Through soul we bless our lives and come to love them in all their moods and aspects.

Using what the spirit has thrown out, soul surrenders to the personal, descending happily into the particulars, as if coming down a grand stair into the swirl of a ballroom. For the soul, what is lost endures like a perfume after the dancer has gone. In the soul's realm we have stories and an imagined life: we have experience, desire, and love.

Soul is weak because it loves—which is of course its strength. Soul is creative: it produces something invisible out of matter. "All love is the love of God," it declares and plunges into the first kiss, into a glass of shiraz, into saving the planet, into eating a bowl of steamed clams, into remodelling the kitchen. Soul connects and loses itself in the connection. It falls and falls; it falls into beauty.

Denser than the spirit, soul gets in the way of the arriving light just enough, delaying it, making it linger. It provides the way for those who have to live in the world and respect it. When the light descends into common things and people—the girl Vermeer painted, the jug we use to pour milk, the letter we write—all, just as they are, with their thick life, are raised toward the gaze of eternity.

Soul's true center is the journey of consciousness—otherwise it can identify no grand principles. Soul doesn't serve other purposes—the taste of life is its own fulfillment. The purpose of a young girl, the purpose of *The Tempest*, the purpose of the coastline of Tasmania, the purpose of fresh grief is revealed in its own being. The point is not to transcend our lives but that our least moment has the royal stain of mortality about it.

Soul brings meaning to experience—including the thoughtful, reflective part of our being, and embracing too what we know most dimly about ourselves, and sometimes shudder at: secret passions and insomnias; helpless, almost indestructible longings; despair and the continuing undercurrent of knowledge that some losses are irretrievable. It brings the possibility of self-knowledge, of an informed compassion and an integrity based on experience. It has its own unique connection with the deep springs of our being.

Soul loves to include and to learn; it is always trying to embrace things, to inhabit the brokenness of the world. Its light is made real by the surrounding dark, its bounty earned by the perilous journey. Soul does not abolish the difficulty of our lives, but brings a music to our pains—its gift is to make us less perfect and more whole.

The Conversation Between Spirit and Soul

Every journey toward wholeness involves the interplay of spirit and soul. Neither is sufficient alone, for we are hybrid beings and cannot confine life to a single purpose. I imagine the conversation between spirit and soul might begin like that of so many couples, with a description of each from the other's point of view. This is more than a summary of the misunderstandings between them. Through showing the weaknesses of each view, we sidle up to a refreshed sense of their necessary virtues.

Soul knows that where spirit is too dominant, we are greedy for pure things: clarity, certainty, and serenity. This may seem harmless at first, or even desirable, but since nothing is wholly pure it leads us to grow heartless with the natural unkemptness of existence, and to think we can make order by imposing rigid rules. Then, inevitably, a shadow grows, until all too often there is a fall into appetites swollen because so long suppressed—this is why we find scandals in the lives of so many religious figures. Spirit forgets the necessity of imperfection, and that within our very incompletion is the opening where love appears. It does not understand the essentially domestic and mortal nature of human life. Identification with the spirit, then, is not the goal of the inner work; such identification can have disastrous consequences because it leads us to think of ourselves as right, as immune from ordinary failings. We have to care for the whole of life, so that spirit does not overwhelm our modest and preserving virtues but finds its proper place, which is central and limited.

On the other hand, spirit knows that soul, in itself, does not have enough of a center. When soul is too dominant, we lose connection with the infinite source and fall under the thrall of the world. Our attention is dispersed into objects and we struggle with the problem of our desire, which renews itself before it is completely satisfied. Soul wanders ever deeper into the marsh of emotion; looking for catharsis, the authentic story, the reason for its pain, it forgets that it can rise.

If soul gives taste, touch, and habitation to the spirit, spirit's contribution is to make soul lighter, able to escape its swampy authenticity, to enjoy the world without being gravely wounded by it. Spirit knows that soul longs to be released from its addictions, its obsession with childhood, its night terrors, and to be able to say good-bye as well as hello, and with something like grace. In the light of the spirit, the tasks of life, profound and small, the labors in which soul is so engaged—from birth to dying, from sex to art, from walking in the city to eating pancakes with maple syrup—are transient and not to be relied on; sacred, but not to be taken too seriously.

Spirit and Soul Outside the Skin

The two powers of soul and spirit are not just inward events—not butterflies imprisoned in the body's cage. While in the main this book describes the individual journey, it is good to remember that soul and spirit also exist beyond us, touching the mountains and streams, bridges, roads, and the ways we teach our children. Between them they bring the glow of life to what we perceive. If a stream is dirty, so is the soul. If a forest is made into a wasteland, so is the spirit lost and disoriented.

Spirit and soul deprivation have different symptoms. The missing sweetness in our cities, the homelessness and choked freeways—these are the public pains of the wounded soul. When we treat ourselves too much as machines, our actions come to bad ends. The worst consequence of the soul's neglect is a lack of love—of our own lives, of each other, of the future, and of the suffering planet. Soul wants time and patience to confer loveliness; it wants to be wooed and longs to find the face of the beloved in the gardens and apartments of the city.

Our panic over death, our helplessness and denial before plagues of the body such as AIDS and our strange post-modern immune disorders—these are symptoms of an exhaustion, a weak connection with spirit. Spirit offers us the possibility of equanimity because it sees suffering as transformation. It knows that shopping doesn't stave off the terror of mortality: only the experience of participating in eternity will set our hearts at rest. Spirit's blessing is its unpredictability and its predilection to descend on the heads of the despised and poor. For spirit, even the rocks and rivers are self, alive and as full of magic as our first love.

We cannot do without either spirit or soul. Our task is to restore the world from our own treasure of inward richness, which, in its subtle and inexorable way, turns outwards to that labor.

Character and Integrity Appear

A great deal of our journey consists of alternating immersion in these two realms, spirit and soul. But if we are to find balance, another level of development is needed. This is the work of *character*. Tempered by the suffering of soul's descent, leavened by the exuberance of spirit's rising, character is the matrix where spirit and soul meet. When we have character, we do not entirely surrender to either spirit or soul, and it is only when neither of these great forces occupies the whole field that they may begin a true conversation in our lives. Then, this very pressure of opposites held in close company gives shape to our uniqueness and freedom. Under the press of these two great forces, the inner life becomes richer, more complex, and less fanatical—we become individual.

What supports character, in turn, is *integrity*. Integrity is the inner sense of wholeness and strength that arises out of our honesty with ourselves; it is the ability to make the right connections and the proper sacrifices, to find a life that is both moral and spontaneous. Character and integrity develop over time. They recognize the soul's pleasure in common life and also the equanimity that comes from a link with the source of things. This is why the actions of a person of character have weight. The Buddhist name for such a person is the Bodhisattva, the one dedicated to inner knowledge for the effects it can bring about in healing the world.

As a culture, we are at a stage in which the lovers of soul and the lovers of spirit are continually doing more of what they already do, meanwhile trying to convert each other. The deficiency in our culture may lie mainly in the realm of the soul, since we absolve ourselves of the soul's public tasks—such as educating the children and caring for the poor and the immigrants. But merely to point out such deficiencies of soul does not achieve wholeness for the culture, and our attempts at remedy often make things worse. We have not yet found out what magic might happen if we were to attend to the paths of both spirit and soul.

This *if* leads to a further picture of the development of the inner life. For when we go beyond the idea of a paleolithic wildness that lies close to the source of life, an image of what we build and cultivate appears. Then the act of inner attention seems to create a medieval walled garden. It is hedged about with silence and stillness, but silence and stillness are not the heart of it. At the center is a fountain and we see that everything has arranged itself around the water playing in the sunlight: here is the source of the timelessness that is everywhere apparent. The more deeply we enter, the more the fountain soars above; awe and wonder claim us. Bear and deer and wallaby; the soldier with his gun; the man with AIDS, hallucinating and skeletal on his deathbed; the child climbing a tree with her tongue thrust out to help her concentrate— all are joined in an incomprehensible and lovely orderliness. The sacred appears in each of life's creatures and the tenderness of this discovery turns us outwards. It asks that we learn how to live, to make a particular path and fullness out of the spirit's eternity and silence.

Claiming the Dark

To learn how to live means claiming more of the territory of life, even, or especially, the darkness. When we begin our inward journey, we think it will be a continuous ascent. But we find that however well we try, we fall into pain, into the excruciating awareness that if we are human we love, and if we love we are vulnerable. The darkness presses hard on us—turbulent, autonomous, full of obsessions and loss. It seems greater than we are and has a mule-like resistance to common sense. As Jung remarked, everything unconscious returns as fate.

If at this time we cling to the spirit, we will think that the fall itself is the problem. Spiritual traditions have a strong tendency to see things this way. The classical solution, then, known in monasteries around the world, is to detach and so cease to suffer. But it is more likely that we pay too little attention to our pain, that we are too eager to clamber back to the cool, pure heights and their certainties. Here, in this human life we share, another kind of spirituality might serve us better: one that sees it is our very losses that save us, by bringing the aspiring spirit downwards and initiating us into soul. This is why the way up—into the true life—begins with the way down.

This revelation of the intimate closeness of beauty and suffering may unbalance our previous idea of order. It tells us that, like Rilke in front of the archaic torso of Apollo, we must change our lives. We must learn to attend more acutely, to grope through the labyrinth, holding the thin twine of spiritual practice as we head into the dark. Through patient observation, then, we find that it is our thoughts and feelings that make us happy or sad, that the quality of our attention changes the colors of the day. This discovery of the reality and then of the consolation of the inner life is our one solution to the problem of suffering, which is also the problem of living up to the underlying, and equally pervading, happiness of life.

Chapter 3

Descent into Night

The First Descent

Midway in the journey of our life
I found myself in a dark wood
DANTE ALIGHIERI

The journey into a life of awareness begins for most of us in a moment of helplessness. When our lives are going well, we do not feel any need to change them, or ourselves. We are content to go on as we are, coasting, serene as planets in their orbits, or caribou on seasonal migration. Our habits of mind are sufficient to sustain us through the days. We are unperturbed, and half asleep.

Then a crisis arrives: a child falls ill, a lover disappoints, or some vast, neutral power of the earth, such as a hurricane or a fire, strips us of everything we have relied upon to stay the same. We will have other descents in life but this first one has a terrifying vividness. Change is sure, and change brings suffering, which is an inner as well as outer event. Under the impact of a crisis, images we have worshipped, beliefs we have cherished, also break and fall away. We lose not only houses, photo albums, and people dear to us, but our idea of what life is. We find ourselves plunging unprepared, a weakness in every limb.

Yet this unexpected fall is also a gift, not to be refused—an initiation ordeal preparing us for new life. The enveloping dark strips us of our sleepyheadedness, our assumption that who we now are and the life we now know will be enough. The night is not interested in our achievements. Pitching headlong into this first descent of the journey, we struggle, we suffer untellable grief, but we also wake up—we begin to see ourselves and our lives for what they are. We cannot return to the way it used to be, even yesterday. We realize that we have no choice: before we can rise up, we must go down and through.

Innocence

> *The unexpected means misfortune from without.*
> *I Ching* (commentary on the hexagram Innocence)

Descending, we leave behind the way we were. Everything we have experienced before this moment is transformed retrospectively into a bedtime story, a pastorale in which actions have no true consequences. It seems that, like Persephone, we have not until now really known loss—that dark soil over which we unthinkingly walked. Now the earth has opened and swallowed us.

We look back, as we always do, through the chasm, and there we see the object of our longing: the blue sky, the white cluster of narcissus, the naive life that is leaving us. For innocence is close to reminiscence. When we have it, we are not aware of it: we long for it only when it is disappearing. The desire to wake up, as from a bad dream; the phrase "If only"; the bargaining with the gods; the yearning to return to the garden even as we are expelled— these thoughts and emotions fix on innocence, the lost, beloved condition.

Innocence belongs to animals, children, forests. It is young, angelic, untouched, vague—the uncarved block of the Taoists, full of possibility because nothing has yet happened. A child watching a river may see and feel that everything flows. She merges with eternity. In this way she lives effortlessly, using the resources of the spirit—she pulls her arms in, kicks her legs out, and up she swings; she breaks sticks into pieces and floats them down the gutter. But her play is something she has found as a gift; nothing of herself has yet been contributed to life and so life, as yet, hardly sticks to her. In Dante's *Divine Comedy*, the unbaptized innocent are assigned a special antechamber of Hell. They do not suffer there, but neither do they taste the joy of Heaven. Innocence is not conscious and does not really worship any god, being itself adrift in eternity. Innocence is not aware of unease, and whatever the soul might interpret as unease and seek causes for, innocence knows only as a blink, a stutter, a moment of interruption that has no story accompanying it. Because innocence is unacquainted with the night, moral choice plays no role in its unfolding.

We see innocence in others as an ideal, and in seeing it this way we can also maintain a certain distance from its beauty, fragility, and otherworldliness, which somehow disturb us. For the word *innocent* has a double always near it—the word *victim*. The Cemetery of the Innocents in Paris was the place where the bones of those who died of the Black Death in the thirteenth century were thrown. Later, in the sixteenth century, Andreas Vesalius, a medical student at the University of Paris, studied these bones in the charnel house where they had been collected. His exploration was the beginning of a movement of consciousness downward, into observation of the dead and away from a learning based solely on ancient texts. Vesalius was to become the founder of modern anatomy—we might say that he brought these innocents back, bone by bone, into the stream of knowledge, making a small piece of soul out of the devastation and ignorance that characterized the medieval plagues.

Like Leonardo da Vinci before him, Vesalius extended his knowledge of anatomy by performing autopsies on corpses stolen from the public gallows. In his illustrations, the gaze of the anatomized is direct. They are not ashamed of being dead or mutilated—it is just their condition. Because he could meet the eyes of the dead, because he *looked for himself*, Vesalius was able to correct the work of Galen—the anatomist of Roman times. And, brought by him into our gaze, the dead rejoin the living, no longer victims, because they participate. Released from the purity conferred by death, they receive from us the honor due to those who have lived out their fate, and we, in turn, are able to learn from them. The achievements of modern medicine depend on this learning.

The fall opens for the innocent the possibility of choice. I think of a woman had been an airy, talented girl, a beauty who studied art but walked within a disorienting clamor of suitors. When she was young, her hallways had been stacked with bouquets. There was a flow of small packages containing diamond earrings and emerald tennis bracelets and once there was a large, mirror-studded cloth elephant. She married one of the senders of beautiful things, and had three children, but no longer cultivated an art beyond her ability, admittedly extraordinary, to reflect back the image of the other before her. Her mother, also a great beauty, had gone mad at the onset of age, starting a new career of imaginative invalidism, and that might have been this woman's fate as well. But then a fortunate thing happened—her husband left.

The woman was helpless at first. Because her husband had been the center of her life, she did not feel her existence had enough weight to continue on its own. She did not know what she wanted, nor had she developed the capacity to stay with a dilemma long enough to make an informed choice. Yet this disaster was also her chance: her loss and her freedom to make a life of her own were the same. Her husband, going off with a younger women to start another family, was perhaps worse off, since he was only repeating the one song he had learned twenty years before. Slowly, painfully, she began to paint, to construct a life of her own, to leave her innocence behind.

The innocent does not learn—for if she does, she has become

experienced. This leads us to the shadowy double of the innocent—the *criminal*, or the *rascal*, who cannot learn consequences. A salesman sells stocks that plummet, but calls up the customer again with a new sure thing, as if the customer were incapable of learning, too. This murky figure is also the *grifter*, the *addict*. Many children steal a little from their mother's purses, perhaps because they do not quite see their mother as a separate being. Most of these children grow up to have their purses raided in turn. But then there is another child, who, mysteriously, doesn't grow up. When he is fifty years old he is still stealing from his mother's purse to buy drugs, still plausibly offering that she might have miscounted or that if not, he is thinking of attending Narcotics Anonymous. Don Juan is another form of this perennial child, pursuing the new, pure love unsullied by familiarity. His promiscuity is a quest against mortality for renewal and yet more renewal, in the hope that everything should be as it was at the beginning of the world. Not yet fallen, he is also not quite human.

But in the end, everyone wants to be human. This is why innocence seems so linked to its opposite, seems to attract the malign powers, and to be complicit in its own undoing. Persephone must rush toward the scented white narcissus blossom and tumble into the chasm that Hades has made, Psyche must listen to her spiteful sisters, light the lamp above the head of Cupid, and destroy the life she knows. Innocence, consciously or not, longs for experience, longs to be different from itself.

Still, how can we fail to treasure our first paradise? As we fall, it is glimpsed by our backward gaze as something not appreciated before it was lost. But we will see it again in another form, for innocence is a foretaste of developed spirituality. And this spirituality draws us and makes us afraid. Innocence is listening to a music that we recollect, but that our daily getting and spending obscure until we can barely make it out. We fear the worldly doom that comes over those who listen too fervently to that music, even as we long to hear it plain and clear. But for now, as we consider the departure of innocence, we must be content to enter consciousness and its journey: a long circumnavigation through darkened lands until we may return, changed, to the effortlessness of the spiritual point of view.

Night's Herald

There is a moment when the fall appears in consciousness, like a new character stepping onstage in a play. Usually we resist such an announcement because it carries with it a terrible pain, but a fall can also be announced by an event we desire. In either case, its distinguishing feature is that it calls our entire life into question. Everything we have believed dissolves beneath us, and we enter a journey whose end we do not know. Whether we recognize this first moment of the journey is not important; it is where it leads us that counts.

Sometimes the herald comes with the trumpets and flags of a great disaster. A woman takes her daughter in for a routine medical exam and learns that her child's persistent earaches are caused by a brain tumor. Another woman, a nurse, is working overseas in a safe, civilized country, when a civil war breaks out and she finds herself accidentally and intimately caught up in the terrifying descent of a whole people. She could leave but does not: instead, accepting the ordeal that fate has offered with such apparent casualness, she crosses the lines to help the wounded of both sides. She goes through the long night of war with the country in which she had been merely a guest before, and afterwards her life too is not the same. In her home she keeps vases and ashtrays made of shell casings, objects that begin to domesticate the time of horror and function too as trophies of initiation. Her sense of the worth of everything human comes from that place.

Descent can also begin with an unexpected reprieve. A young soldier, a scout in a jungle in Asia, looked up one afternoon and saw an enemy platoon on the opposite hill. He realized that they had been sitting there for some time, that they could have killed him but had not. He and they watched each other, without thought, as animals might. Then the enemy soldiers filed quickly away, without cover, disappearing over the hill. The soldier in turn did not fire. By the time he came home, he was no longer able to believe in the war he had volunteered for. His children will tell their children that story of a moment of supreme life in the jungle. If a nurse in the civil war discovered how dangerous relatives can be to each other, the soldier found that even enemies can have an incomprehensible fellow feeling. Each experience led to a painful reassessment of life and its meaning.

Sometimes there is not a clear moment when the fall begins; there is just a thickening of life's energy, as if a person had been sleeping on a hillside, and awoke to find the weather changed, the landscape unfamiliar, and wild beasts approaching. That is Dante's story, and it is common in a life that is otherwise peaceful. A man realizes his wife has drifted away into an interior place inaccessible to him, that his long marriage is probably ending, and that his children are strangers to him. He does not know where the divide began; he was busy working and doing what he thought good. Yet now when he looks at his family across a table there is a chasm, and it seems as if a cold wind is blowing in a room that was previously so familiar as not to be noticed.

Sometimes the trumpet sounds when the story is already far along. A minister whose father had been the town drunk shielded his son from the grandparents and tried to rear him in innocence. But the son didn't understand the accumulation of pain and knowledge behind the father's rules, and at seventeen, went off to live in the streets and take drugs. The son had never been initiated, we might say, and so needed to enter the very realms from which his father had tried so hard to protect him. Then the boy's mother noticed that she too was in pain. She had known this in a vague way before, but had thought it a dark music for her ears only. Until her son left, it didn't occur to her that her own sense of suffocation was important. Children are surprisingly impervious to the intentions of their parents, so we can't say that the parents set their son on his dangerous course. But it did seem that the boy's plunge signalled that it was past time to attend to a familial darkness long ignored.

Not only individuals but whole nations can slip into the abyss.

The war in Vietnam crept up on American culture, announced little by little in small-town deaths. Few people thought that sending military advisers into that then remote and little-heard-of country was a matter for moral questioning. In this way a small hubris, if there is such a thing, became a great evil. The assassinations of John F. Kennedy and Martin Luther King were large announcements of the general climate of confusion, of pain to come, as well as, in King's case, a declaration that old evils are hard to set at rest.

In the 1980s, suspicion of government and the pleasant dream of reducing taxes, ideas unremarkable in themselves, and in some degree consequences of the failed war in Southeast Asia, led to an astonishing heaping up of debt and a general refusal of the obligations of citizenship. The result of these unexamined ideas was a great deterioration in civil life.

The heralding moment awakens us to the bitter potion of sorrow in the world. We may think of the first traumatic summons as the darkness itself, but it is merely the first shock, an announcement of pain to come and of the journey through it. After we have heard that call, there is no choice: we have already bitten into the apple of the knowledge of good and evil and we are becoming human, with the inevitable labor and blessings that follow.

The legend of Shakyamuni, the historical Buddha, illustrates some of the complexity of our response to the herald of night. At his birth, it was prophesied that he would become a king or a great sage. His parents, royalty themselves, wanted him to be king; they taught him the arts a prince must know, they found him a bride. They tried to protect him from the harshness of the world, assuming that if he discovered what life is really like, he would flee along the path of wisdom. Still, unawareness is not always easy to preserve; one day, upon leaving the palace, he saw a sick person, an old person, and a corpse. These three revelations of the actual were enough; the discovery of suffering and its inevitable course broke the spell of his innocence. Then he saw an ascetic and recognized that here was a way to address the sharpness that had come over him. He began a long journey downwards in which he left his palace and family and nearly starved to death in the forest. The realization of pain in the world always has personal consequences: it affects *me*, and *my* child and *my* job; it is the plan for *my* life that is ruined.

The legendary prince didn't wait for disaster to overtake him in order to do something about his unconscious condition. He set off, bending his life toward prayer and meditation. Yet taking action in the face of suffering is not simple. The quantity of darkness in this tale is large, and holds the possibility of getting lost forever: Shakyamuni abandoned his family. It is said that on the night he left, he paused in the doorway in silent farewell to the woman and child sleeping there, and didn't dare to wake them. If we imagine their confusion when they woke the next morning, we see that if the man has found a sure path, he has asked his family to bear the desolation and loss that is the underside of his certainty. A child needs more than food and shelter—a child needs stories and reasons and caresses, the knowledge of a father and a mother, the presence of history.

By leaving the child and the woman, Shakyamuni conformed

to the familiar pattern that for the sake of developing the spirit, we must turn away from the world and our ties. The same gesture appears in Jesus' rejection of his mother. But this means to turn away also from the trees and the fate of the planet and the soul, which loves these things. If we are to have a marriage of soul and spirit, we will have to find a way to walk back eventually through the charged doorway and find the wisdom of the sages in that small, quiet room where the woman and her child are sleeping still.

Initiation

When our innocence is gone, and the descent has become irrevocable, the mind becomes for a while very open. This inner fluidity arises from the ordeal of our suffering, which strips away our usual ways of dealing with the world. Such a state of mind is valued and cultivated both in high spiritual traditions and by hunter-gatherers; it allows a through-passage for messengers from the world beyond temple, village, and campfire. In the mind of openness, infinity comes near, and with help, we can find a link to our ancestors, a way to participate in the world of wild animals, of rivers and stars. This is the inner, transitional space of initiation. When we enter it, we move from being victims of fate to being pilgrims on a path.

All inner change seems to involve entering an initiation space in which we move temporarily from the center to the margins of life. In tribal cultures, initiation includes a formal, controlled method of thrusting the initiate into an overwhelming darkness and then leading him back out into a new connection with the community. The process is usually composed of an ordeal, an inner shift of some kind, and a reunion on different terms with the community of the living.

All cultures devise ordeals for children on the verge of growing up. As well as being arduous, a good ordeal should teach the initiate something about being an adult. War and military training have always served as harsh initiations for young men and for the civilians whom war rolls over. In a peaceful time, exams, irregular French verbs, differential calculus, driving tests, football games, and piano recitals can provide a form of ritual transition. Less official initiations exist as well—drinking, drug-taking, first sex, drag racing, ecstatic plunges into music and poetry—and seem to center around altering the consciousness given by childhood. Childbirth is a common initiation for young women, holding the traditional elements of pain and danger, connection to the natural processes of life, and winning through to a new identity within the community. Uncontrolled and terrifying ordeals are our common fate too—earthquake, fire, rape, and street fights; the sudden death of childhood friends; a car turning over and over on a Saturday night, its lights illuminating a cornfield, the sky, the road, the cornfield again.

The traverse out of the innocence of childhood can be so dangerous that some peoples have developed particularly fierce forms to contain the energy. Aboriginal boys in Australia were, and sometimes still are, taken from the tribe by the old men and subjected to long ordeals in which they learned to manage hunger and thirst, as part of their instruction in the secrets of hunting, history, and ceremony. Their chests and penises were cut open to mark them as having been changed into men. The idea animating these rites is that the world produces our bodies, but we are not fully human until the elders have helped make our souls.

Although the paradigmatic rite of passage occurs at adolescence, initiation and its ordeals are not confined to a particular time of life. Every descent offers the possibility of initiation, and, as Dante noticed, there is often a descent in the middle of life. The ordeal itself—whether or not we have elders to guide us through it—purifies. It is raw torment and we must bear it, that is all—and yet, within the framework of the inner life, torment is also a door, a gate, an entrance exam, testing the depth of our sincerity and commitment.

At first we have to stay with our suffering without hope of change. We do not know it, but endurance itself provides us with the weight to bear the next steps. A woman who lost her only child, a daughter, was still grieving eighteen months later. The books she found in her desperation said she was supposed to be pulling out of it, but she wasn't, and how can there be a program for such sorrow? One night she dreamed:

I am tramping through the night, tramping and tramping.

That is all there was to the dream and all there was to her life at that moment—to march as if she were in an army, and to bear what she had to bear and to go where she was being led. Each morning she woke up with the presence of her daughter and each morning had to talk herself into living through the day. She hardly dared to think or feel; breathing and walking were all she could do. She had no sense that this terrible time would ever end.

Still, when an image of the ordeal appears, as in this dream, then there is some possibility of change, because a story is starting to take form. A little piece of what we shall later recognize as soul-making is going on. An image offers us the beginning of a relationship with the inner life. Its appearance tells us that the dreamer, the story maker, is still alive. But this women's dream is so terse, laconic, and concrete that the numbing effects of her ordeal are also plain. There is not much consolation from such a dream; it is a thin shaft of light in an enormous dungeon.

An ordeal doesn't gain meaning until it begins to lighten. At first we are just reduced, like apricots being boiled into jam. We lose the upper levels of consciousness and are sunk in personal griefs. As we descend, there are no obvious edges to darkness, we are taken downwards and further downwards, into the deeper night.

The Destruction of the Images

We depend on our images as they depend on us. In World War II, paintings were plundered by the Nazis and carried off along with their previous owners into slavery. In this way the thieves tried to capture the record of the soul's history and the promise of the spirit. Those who wish to harm us often try to gain power over us by capturing or altering our images. In the ancient Middle East, statues of former kings were often defaced. In China, during the Cultural Revolution, images that held the ancient continuity of the culture—antique scrolls, old porcelain, the mummified bodies of sages dead a thousand years—were indiscriminately plundered and destroyed. Not only can our most precious images be broken, we can also be deceived by the glamour of untrue images, which need to be broken as Moses destroyed the golden calf. In the Trojan War, the Greeks triumphed by offering a false image—the great horse that turned out to be full of soldiers was an image the Trojans should have destroyed. What's more, the Greeks claimed that the horse was a kind of reparation for their earlier theft from the Trojans of an image from the shrine of Athena, layering a false representation upon a theft.

The force of images is also destroyed when they are co-opted and stripped of their meaning—swastikas used as earrings by kids who haven't heard of Hitler, crucifixes on décolletage without any sense that the transgression is religious. Advertisements in *The New Yorker* that feature models whom the Greeks would have recognized as Persephone and Hades, though they would have been curious about the tango that has interlocked their legs, or as Ares sneaking off for the weekend with Aphrodite while her husband is at work, often seem exciting but curiously without nourishment. They lack heft because they link us only to an outer satisfaction—it is implausible to our souls that we should become Zeus just by the purchase of a chariot made by Lexus. So we are tempted but do not link to a sense of anything greater than ourselves. Spirit is missing and soul cannot quite believe.

Genuine descent breaks our old life. In the personal realm, the destruction of our images is one of the things that gives our surrender a devastating force. The woman who lost her child lost her imagined path into the future—her daughter's high school graduation, her daughter's career and marriage, and her own grandchildren. And with the loss of the future, the past became fixed, and supersaturated. When we lose our images, we lose our dreams and our gods, lose both what we worship and the direction in which we pray.

At such times, we may find ourselves trapped for long periods in the new images of nightmare, but this is not the worst fate. For without the dark images, the dream life and the life of art may shut down, leaving us numb. The first route can be seen in Goya's terrible and fascinating paintings of the dead and wounded of Napoleon's Spanish campaign, and in Picasso's *Guernica*. Paul Celan's dark poetry and Primo Levi's autobiographical accounts of the Holocaust take this path too. Yet even a great artist may fail to heal the images and so the life; both these writers killed themselves and so can be counted among the Holocaust dead. Veterans who wake shaking and yelling twenty years after they have been in combat are still caught in the images of nightmare, trying to live them through, to dream their way into wholeness.

The response of numbness and silence can be seen in those who say that you cannot write about the Holocaust, the terror of the Khmer Rouge, the genocide of Rwanda, since they are catastrophes too great to be described. To do so, goes the thought, is to do so inadequately and so to fail the victims yet again. Some survivors of great trauma suffer from blindness of no known physical cause, and this blindness too is perhaps a kind of turning away from something sacred, tormenting and unendurable. The loss of songs, the loss of languages of tribes, which themselves have disappeared, the dumbness of the defeated and even of the vanishing natural world—these are inarticulate responses to our domination by night.

The grieving mother tramping through the night of her dreams marches at the edge of silence. Her dream does not touch on the terrible loss, the time in the bone marrow transplant ward, the mutilation of surgery, the hemorrhages, the massive dose of morphine on the last night or the sweet, searing conversations with the child's school friends. Still, this terse dream is not quite dumb; at least it offers an image of her struggle when all other images have been taken away.

During the descent we also lose the way others see us. This is not always a bad thing in the long run, but it is humiliating and painful. The mask that we present to the world slips off and the face behind it becomes visible, with its expression of terror, greed, despair, dishonesty—whatever is usually kept in the cellar. The moment of surrendering the old image—of life, of the self—is most painful. At such a time we know that we must strike out on our own, but in our new solitude and shame sometimes we go under, for a while, or forever. Nonetheless, the stripping away of the mask that links us to all that we are known to be and do is a necessary part of the descent, one that eventually allows a fresh start.

One optimistic old tale shows the value of destroying the

images: A ragged Zen teacher was travelling in winter and at the end of the day came to a temple where he was invited to stay overnight. Outside, the snow was piled high and the cold bitter. In the middle of the night, the traveller took down the altar figure and set it on fire to keep warm. The caretaker came running in to protest. The teacher asked whether the ashes would have the pearl-like relics that a Buddha's ashes are supposed to contain. "No, no," said the caretaker, "it's just made of wood." "Then why don't you come and warm yourself," said the teacher.

This story is prized in the Zen tradition: It describes the way our images tend to ossify, and sometimes need to die. It is as if all warmth has been locked up in the image. Only when it is destroyed can life be sustained. When our old images break we suffer terribly, but then, when all goes well, new light and heat bring companionship and a humble knowledge of the real.

True and False Suffering

Freud, among others, pointed out that there is true and false suffering. The breaking of the images abolishes our false pain and makes way for the true to appear. False suffering is a defense against the vigor and tumult of experience. Our true suffering is the shared lot of humanity. We love and want to be loved in return, we have to eat when we are hungry, we thrive on a freedom from danger that is rare. These are the needs of life. Yet they are uncertain. War strides over cities; famine, earthquake, and illness ravage us. Our false suffering appears when we add unnecessary pains to our necessary ones—when we become suspicious and cruel because our affection has not been returned, when we become greedy because we were hungry once, when we envy those who do things better than we do. If our hurt becomes a consuming passion for revenge, a necessary suffering has grown pathological. There are times when we take the true, irritating pain of life and build a strange pearl around it, a symptom that seems to an outsider aesthetically interesting but fundamentally redundant. There is the woman who, in her quest for perfection, must eat a pound of chocolate at supper and throw up before bedtime, or the man who, rebellion and achievement having found a stasis in his soul, refuses to complete his doctoral dissertation but remains a student all his days. Descent refines us so that our pain becomes more and more authentic. As we flee it less, it touches us more terribly and more intimately; we grow interested in the pain that is so interested in us. True suffering is modest—it doesn't mean things, it *is* things.

A woman discovered that her boyfriend had had an affair. Before that moment she hadn't even been sure she cared about the man. But now she did care. "Either it's all going to break into pieces," she said, "or we're going over the waterfall together, we're going far deeper into the relationship than we intended. Either way is terrifying." And either way she would have more life. To find out how delicate her emotions were and how much she wanted the relationship to go on was itself worthwhile. Her helplessness was more interesting than her indifference had been, was becoming even more interesting than the relationship. She now understood that her experience mattered—her raw pain, her hopes, the stuff of her days.

True suffering drives us into new regions. If we escape from our suffering too easily or by sleight of hand, we are disappointed. We feel that we have evaded some challenge, missed the gift in the pain. It is as if destiny had not marked us for anything real and we merely scurry at the edges of life. Henry James in his story "The Beast in the Jungle" tells the tale of a man who realizes at last that his "great destiny" was that nothing would happen to him and that he had failed to notice the woman who loved him. Rilke, in the original version of the Tenth Duino Elegy, put it like this,

> . . . How dear you will be to me then, you nights
> of anguish. Why didn't I kneel more deeply to accept you,
> inconsolable sisters, and, surrendering, lose myself
> in your loosened hair. How we squander our hours of pain.
> How we gaze beyond them into the bitter duration
> to see if they have an end. Though they are really
> seasons of us, our winter-
> enduring foliage, ponds, meadows, our inborn landscape,
> where birds and reed-dwelling creatures are at home.

Betrayal

However inevitable our downward journey, when we are pitched into night and its suffering we feel aggrieved: everything we relied on has been snatched away. Many religions have myths of betrayal at their core—Judas, we are told, sold Jesus for silver, the

Buddha survived an assassination attempt, and Osiris was murdered by his brother. Such stories help us to accommodate to our own losses. With the death of the founder of a religion, the light seems to have withdrawn back into the realm it came from, leaving the people without warmth and direction. The grief of that huge absence asks for an answer, an explanation. To blame Judas for the death of Jesus, for example, is to become like the husband who blames the singer in the band for stealing his wife.

A sense of having been betrayed makes a pattern of the enormity of our grief. Survivor guilt seems to have the same purpose. A man whose wife died of a heart attack reacted by blaming himself. He went over and over the day of the death, watching her fall on the grass beside an oak tree, running to her, picking her up, checking for breathing. The loss was truly out of his control, but he felt driven to find out what his error had been. His thought returned again and again to his guilt like an animal coming to shelter. The guilt restored a sense of order to a torn world. As he said, "If I am to blame, at least someone is responsible."

This hunger for a comprehensible pattern is the source of the feeling of intimacy and complicity that sometimes appears between betrayer and betrayed. The sense of having been betrayed and the sense of having done wrong are very close. A woman has decided to end a long marriage because she feels that she is not seen or respected enough. Indeed, her husband is a bully, belittling the children, smashing furniture when things don't go his way. But at the same time, she has been trying to conceive a baby and thinks she might be pregnant. As Borges said, love is a religion with a fallible god. Each of her feelings is a betrayal of its opposite—her marriage is a betrayal of herself, her desire to end the marriage a betrayal of family.

Many times it seems that there is no way to move forward in our lives except through betrayal. Along with our suffering comes an awakening to contradiction, a discovery that we can no longer be quite sure of our motives or even our intentions. And so we love, we collude in our own betrayal.

Death itself is a kind of forgetting, an infidelity. The planet forgets us, just as we are unfaithful to our first love. Betrayal tells us that the world is capacious and strange, more dangerous and more fascinating than we had thought. Life has seduced us and we shall, no doubt, die of this seduction. Yet it is marvelous too, and if we do not let ourselves be seduced by existence, there is nowhere for the fingers of eternity to seize us.

The positive side of betrayal is that it affirms life—last season's cornstalks are plowed under and feed the crop that is yet to be. To grow up, a child has to turn away from childhood, to betray her life of toys, her sense of family. We can be too loyal to our suffering. Sometimes we need also to forget it, to betray or neglect even our own knowledge. We can be holders of a private knowledge: that a woman has already decided to leave, for example, and we see her husband holding a loaf of bread as if it were a violin, heading toward a warm glow that will not be at the kitchen table when he actually arrives but which nevertheless has an existence now, as he inhales the bread, and before he has heard the news. And we see a child running between trees in the twilight with his friend. He ignores the call to dinner; cannot hear anything, cannot see anything but the sound and illumination of his happiness—while we know, we have seen the charts, that he will die of leukemia.

At such a moment we can find unbearable the juxtaposition of innocence and suffering to come, the thought that the happiness in question is entirely illusory. It can seem that to have our impotent and piercing knowledge is somehow to be an accomplice of pain. Yet from the point of view of an angel, we are all like the man carrying bread, the boy in the twilight: when a child is born, the angel knows that at age five she will be run over by a truck; as the bride is throwing her bouquet, the angel sees her death in childbirth. It is not that as T. S. Eliot said, humankind cannot bear very much reality, but that it is hard to have the grand view of the angel at the same time as we have the intimate view of the man who wants supper with his family, of the boy who wants to run and run forever instead of coming in to supper. We have to acknowledge that the man and the child were happy, looking forward to a future that would not be theirs; we have to say that life itself is beautiful before we talk about outcomes. Everything we taste is snatched from death: our responsibility is to taste it completely. We betray the angel's view because we must. Those we love die, yet we must eat, we must sing, we must love them anyway—that is our job. We may have the angel's view as well as the child's, but not instead of it. When we stop singing, it is our time, and we too go into the dark.

We cultivate the feeling of betrayal, embed its stories in the founding tales of our religions, because the experience of betrayal is one way that we can relish the dark and honor its possibilities—

at a slight angle, so to speak, without quite admitting what we do. The role of victim is a solution to the indignities and grief of being human, a role that makes us, for the time of its duration, more than mortal. It is not enough to suffer. There are costumes and arias, recruitment to the cause and public swooning. What we have lost is always our connection to Heaven; we have been driven down into matter. Making an image of betrayal, worshipping it, actually allows us to plunge, to go with the dark, desperate and exhilarated, while still saving face. When we grasp hold of betrayal it carries us deeper into night, toward despair—for the labyrinth that it reveals has no escape, and no windows, and no one is waiting outside, holding the other end of a cord.

The Monster Despair

> *The specific character of despair is precisely this:*
> *it is unconscious of being despair.*
>   SØREN KIERKEGAARD

Night grows thicker, and we sink in our journey to the valley of despair. The descent is almost accomplished now. In *despair*, we know the stripping away of hope. If we define despair as fundamental ignorance (as Kierkegaard does), then we can imagine it as a kind of fusion with the foggy mass of night, and so an absence of the shapeliness of things. Despair offers no images or shrines, it is inert and motionless, without color or scent.

Within this amorphous fusion, we do not feel connected to life, but oppressed by its muddy swirling. The Buddhist explanation of despair is that it comes from alienation, from not under-standing our relationship to the wellsprings, from not understand-ing that we have the same nature as the trees, the rocks, and the people around us—kin, friend, and foe—and, like them, are sus-tained by the invisible source. In Christianity, despair appears via the doctrine of original sin, as banishment from our true home. In Judaism, too, it stems from our condition of exile: the Messiah, the one who is complete, is perpetually arriving, but not yet quite here. Each tradition shows that despair is a separation from the light and at the same time a fusion with the dark.

Despair is a time of waiting, of paralysis, of non-time. When we are in its kingdom we do not distinguish among things. Our experience is incomplete because it is non-experience; it is not any-thing in particular itself and neither is it turning into something else. In psychiatric diagnostic manuals, despair is called depres-sion, as if it were a weather system. The lists of symptoms describe vegetative signs: slowness of speech, inability to attend, indiffer-ence to pleasure—as if a person turned into a plant, became pas-sive and rooted, wrapped in winter fog, lacking animal spirits. The danger in despair is often greatest as a person starts to emerge—only then does he realize that what he has been experiencing is an-guish and only then does he have enough energy to kill himself.

Despair is a pit beyond any explanation. Melancholy, midlife anxiety, chronic illness are only a part—such occasions may be present, but then other people experience the same troubles and do not fall into despair. So despair is an experience in itself, one of the true moments of life. Despair is the experience among all others that is incomplete, something that has not yet become itself, a creature not yet formed out of the murk and waters. A woman dreamed:

> I am walking on the edge of a great ocean but I can hardly see it. There is fog all around. I can barely see my feet on the beach.

Perhaps this is the greatest pain—not to have a story, not to have reasons, and to have only an image of the lack of images—fog and the sea, barely visible.

Despair is the point where the descent slows, where we enter the darkness proper in which we are not really falling but drifting. In the abyss, we approach the heart of the night. Innocence has departed. The images that sustained us or confined us have been broken. The way of life, the compromises and pleasures that we trusted to see us through, have vanished, and we have fallen into the thickest confusion. The torment and secret gift of deepest night is our next subject.

| # Love in the Dark Time

Dyed and Stained All Through with Night

Thickest night is fascinating because we are so afraid of it. The terrible intensity of descent itself can be a kind of fulfillment. Men wake in a sweat remembering a battle of fifty years ago, but along with the terror, they can feel a secret love of the heightened life of that time, when each moment was lived at the edge of death. Much of what we do in the descent can be explained only if we recognize that it has its own gravity: the darkness pulls us into itself until it finds its pure form. When the night is not complete, we are driven to darken it further, until we are stained and dyed all through. Then the dark becomes a kind of lover: we keep company with it for its own sake, learn how to move in its hard, narrow bed, to find the warmth in it, to let it restore us. We do this by darkening the darkness.

Darkening the Darkness

If I defer the grief I will diminish the gift.
EAVAN BOLAND

Darkening the darkness need not be done consciously—night will come to us of its own accord. But perhaps it eases us to have a map: to know that, whether by fate or by our own act, night deepens and the ordeal of our initiation becomes more thorough. Darkening always has the edge of something uncontrollable about it. This is what makes it terrifying and fascinating. Yet without this edge it couldn't function; what hasn't truly gone down cannot rise.

Descent often begins with loss and the realization of mortality; so illness, funerals, and memorials can be the occasions for our darkening. The body's fragility is intimate with its delight and we are driven, as if by a duty, to discover what kind of dying is right for us and what kind of mourning is proper for the dead. To do this is part of the work of the dark time.

The traditional Buddhism of South Asia takes on this task through a saturation with images of the body's impermanence. The most beautiful of us will soon be wrinkled. Teeth fall out, breasts sag, we end up with prostate surgery and hysterectomies. Students of impermanence go out at night and meditate in graveyards, steeping themselves in the truth that is evident there. They imagine themselves dying, losing their faculties one by one. They imagine a beautiful partner, and then imagine this lovely being aged, decrepit, dying, and rotting. This may sound macabre, but it is undertaken in service of awareness. To dissolve ourselves into the dark loosens us, frees us of our common terror. We develop our attention to such a level that it can hold us in every circumstance, including all the ragged events of the soul's domain, including even the prospect of our own inevitable dissolution.

The meditation upon darkening need not be consciously intended. Whenever we turn toward the wellspring we call up the night. A man I know used to go blind during meditation retreats. He couldn't see his hands and friends would have to lead him around for a day or so until the condition would clear up by itself. While, finally, he found a doctor who gave him a physiological explanation, there is also a certain emblematic beauty to his symptom. The Zen teacher Koun Yamada used to say that by sweeping the mind clear, meditation takes away false blindness and gives us true blindness. Spiritual work brings us down to the foundations of life before it lets us rise.

Here is another story of darkening—a memorial service for a young professional woman. Her many friends gathered at her house. Some people did performance pieces, some read poems, some talked to the dead woman; almost everyone drank. At one point her husband grew agitated and began shouting her name— an event both complicated and raw, in which elements of Job-like accusation of God seemed to combine with a movement toward the dead woman. A few of those present became very angry, accusing him of ruining the ceremony and also of other old grievances they held. One young man lost his temper completely and attacked the widower; a window was shattered. I remember lying on the carpet alongside the grieving man, holding him and shielding him at the same time, while he went on murmuring to his dead wife. Almost everyone left; then the few who remained sat on the bed and read Dylan Thomas aloud. This quiet act of attention reknitted the soul of the evening and transformed its unravelling into something striking, survivable, and even necessary.

What had happened to make such disorder? Death had called to the man, and he had listened, walking a little way beside it, keeping company with the uncompanionable. It was as if his sorrow had breached the veil between worlds, drawing the mourners into a border place where the dead swirl around and grief is like a high wind. Then, with the breaking of the window, the fit that was in everyone passed: the grieving man toppled back to the floor and lay there. For the moment, enough of a sacrifice had been made. Thomas's poetry brought the human connections, which had seemed frail, back again.

Darkening—exhilarating, terrifying—takes us farther into Hell. Sometimes the irreducible darkness pulls us in; sometimes we rush toward it in an active and self-destructive fashion. At such a moment it is as if we can't have enough of it, we want to be saturated in the primeval simplicity of night, of being a mortal body—full of sensation and near to death.

Poison: The Perverse and the Strange

Darkening is work on behalf of the soul and so it goes against our passion for light and spirit—an air of paradox clings to our descent. One Buddhist teaching story tells that the peacock's feathers are bright because it eats a poison it then transmutes into lovely colors. That is how soul works: by taking in poison and twistedness, we move the dark matter of our lives toward beauty and connection.

Masochism, in the sense of a certain fascination with and ecstatic transformation of suffering, is a regular feature of the path. The reason for this is simple. Life makes us suffer and at the same time gives us an obligation to relish it. To suffer, then, is to taste life. The descent develops our passive, dreaming capacity, our acceptance of whatever comes as fate. We can see this universal stance at work most clearly in its most literal form—with someone who actually seeks punishment.

The release of masochism lies first in its quest for the certainties of transgression, punishment, and forgiveness. A man knocks on a door and, when it opens, he is blindfolded and bound and made to wait; then he is whipped while being lectured about his imaginary transgressions. A senior executive, he finds it a relief to be free of command, to be wrong, to be humiliated, to have someone else in charge. There is another pull to masochism as well. Through pain we are released from the burden of consciousness; the physicality of suffering breaks through our alienation and ensures our participation in our own lives. And this theater does not belong only to the person with eccentric sexual taste, it is also the shape of love for the senior partner in a law firm whose wife throws such excoriating tantrums that he goes to work each day with ever-deeper shadows under his eyes while—ever more abject—he asks her permission for the most trivial actions. In masochism, great forces move us about and their power makes the universe, for the moment, comprehensible and the most eccentric rules just. A world charged with causes is full of importance. Even its pains are reassuring.

Suffering can confer belonging, moral relief, and superiority. The wolf that cringes and shows its throat is not attacked and has a place, albeit a low one, in the pack. We also have a temptation to claim the status of victim even when, to outsiders, we do not seem to have earned it, because to be a victim is both a plea and a special fate—a stance the soul may take before the impenetrable gaze of eternity.

The perverse also appears in the flaws in our mentors. Part of being in the night is that even the guides there seem to be damaged. The heroes of the spirit, like those of the outer world, have their devouring madnesses, their paranoias and secret midnight trysts. The surprises and scandals of spiritual life are part of its movement toward soul, as interesting and as necessary to it as the magic.

Zen is a tradition known for its warrior style and robust attitude toward the inner life, yet one morning the monks at the great temple of Nanzenji in Japan came in for their meditation and found, in the dim light before dawn, a bundle hanging from the rafters: their master, dead. People whispered—could it be that he was not enlightened? But that is a question impossible to answer. That teacher has passed beyond our explanations, our hopes, and even our forgiveness; he has set out on his own long journey, whither we do not know, and his action has become a source for our own painful curiosity about the costs of being too close to the spirit, as Icarus came too close to the sun.

Closer to home, a famous Christian preacher, a man whose whole theme was to preach against lust, was found to patronize prostitutes. For his followers, no doubt, this was a dreadful betrayal, but at the same time, he becomes for us all a figure more complicated, sympathetic, nearer to the dark and its possibilities of growth. The vices of the great are dear to us. Exposed, they evoke envy, rage, loathing, and disappointment. We can see that they have not transcended the darkness we had hoped they would lead us beyond—the concealment and shabby floundering between the public and private realms.

Our highest ideals are always being betrayed because they belong to the realm of the perfect spirit, and no mere human can hold them for long. But the failures have their virtue too, drawing public people into community with us, making them recognizable: no longer monuments, they are revealed now as sharers with us of the secret, excruciating places of initiation. These accounts offer the harsh poetry of the night journey, showing how much despair there is for residue even among the great, and also how much comedy—which is what we are left with when the heroes go astray.

Fever cures fever, a thief catches a thief, and we fight a forest fire by back-burning toward it. A snake winds around the healing staff of Aesculapius, the ancient god of medicine, where it can still be seen today etched into the glass doors of medical clinics.

Aesculapius was said to have access to the blood from the deadly gorgon Medusa. Blood from the left arm killed people, but he could use a drop of blood from the right arm to bring the newly dead back to life.

So, with our inner poisons, the toxins can be the mode of cure. Here is a dream about the homeopathy of the spiritual and physical life. The dreamer was a successful professional woman whose emotions, in reaction to a physical illness, had grown volatile and tormented.

> I am in a jungle setting. I'm observing a medical practice
> where they are attaching a snake to a child's chest to draw
> the poison out. The snake is bright, bright green, striped,
> very long and undulating.

The green snake of the dream, like the jungle, is full of energy, the wave form of life. The image tells us we can find a passage deeper into the emotions and fevers that make us sick, into a clearing in the inner wilderness where the cure is to be bitten by life.

Servitude: Marriage to the Night

Whether fate carries us off or we actively seek the night, a time comes when we identify with the dark, however involuntarily— when we marry and serve it. At such periods, we may intensify our sorrows, as if to find a way through. The ancient myth describing this moment is the story of the maiden Persephone. At play in the spring fields, she found an irresistible, glorious, fragrant, hundred-headed narcissus flower called up by her grandmother, the Earth Goddess. But as Persephone ran to pluck it, a chasm opened in the earth, and Hades, God of the Underworld, came with his chariot and plunging horses and bore her down into his silent realm. Her mother, Demeter, mourned so terribly—in our language, became so depressed—that the survival of the earth was threatened and Persephone was allowed to return into the light of day. But while in the underworld she had eaten seven pomegranate seeds from Hades' marble table, and so each winter she must spend a portion of her year ruling with him, as Queen of the Dead.

The myth shows us in our first innocence and shows also how that innocence needs to be carried off by life. The Earth Goddess sets the plot going by summoning up, as a potter draws clay into form, an irresistible flower. But Persephone participates too, as we all do. She eats the food of that dark place beneath, as we do also, accepting mortality as the cost of incarnation.

We can see the same inner energies in a story of contemporary life. A woman was married to a man who ruined holidays and birthdays with his irrational and violent behavior. He blamed her for things beyond her control and occasionally hit her. They were nearly always short of money. Her friends told her to leave him, and she would for a while, when he hurt her, but she always had her reasons for going back. One night she dreamed a simple dream:

> I am in an underground parking garage. A gangster comes along in a limousine. The car stops, the door opens. I climb in, and we drive off.

Here there is a wrong union in the inner life, a continuing condition. In Hades' palace—the underground parking garage, place of shootouts and lurking stalkers, she gets in the car with the god of death, the stranger who seems eternally familiar. Her decision to go with the gangster, to stay in the marriage, seemed to be in service of her longing to be constrained by a fierce power, to intensify the night. Her friends lectured her and grieved, just like Persephone's mother. But nothing seemed to be shifting: she was still eating pomegranate seeds in the house of her dark lord, and not yet ready for spring. When someone is in Hell and they cannot understand reason, all we can give them is the kindness of our attention, and our sorrow, and the telling of their story.

Sometimes we seem to relive in a dramatic form the darkness of past trauma, to descend with full consciousness into the night we have known in the past, but not fully experienced. A woman grew up in a moderately successful Hollywood household, which beneath meticulous appearances of happiness and beauty held a dark secret: her father had been sexually involved with her younger sister from the time the girl was three. The woman had protested but, a child herself at the time, was helpless to change the situation. She had complex emotions about her memories—grief, rage, and even a feeling of not being chosen. Her first suicide attempt came when she was a young teenager. For years, then, she spent each day trying not to kill herself. As she emerged from this terrible time she began to run with motorcycle gangs. She rode a big, fast bike and pumped iron. She learned the martial arts. If we read this time of her life as we would a poem, it was as if she had accepted a role as Persephone in the underworld, lowering her consciousness. There are shamans who dream that they are animals in the world below, and Lucius, the hero of *The Golden Ass*, was turned into a donkey, forced to know the darkness of animal life. She seemed to be making a performance piece out of the painful ingredients given her by the world she grew up in. She was drenching herself in the same desperation, but visibly, publicly, without pretense of beauty or happiness. Certainly she was often close to death. Those who loved her could do nothing but worry and hold her in their awareness and wait the time through, taking on the role of Demeter.

Eventually, dawn came with its gray light, and the fever seemed to break. She became able to weep. She went off to graduate school. But she was like a nineteenth-century explorer come back among the clubs in London, still with the traces of tropical illness on her face and tribal markings on her arms. Normality never seemed quite able to claim her: her fierceness, her muscles, the curious originality of her thought all seemed to say, "Though I walk among you like this, I have lived a long time in the night, and it has marked me, and, as you see me now, so I am." While she found joy, she never forgot the night and, like Persephone, seemed always to commit part of her year and part of herself to the underworld.

The First Surrender

At the bottom of the descent we surrender because we have no other choice. This has nothing to do with surrender to a human agency: like Job, we are falling ever deeper into matter, which is indifferent to our wishes, our blandishments, and our intelligence, and which overwhelms us. The only experiment possible is to experience life's raucous, grinding force at work upon us. At such a moment, no one voice speaks in consciousness—there is a babble, a multiplicity of fragments. Terror may intensify to the point where consciousness disintegrates. Then even the healing elements may betray us—we may dream of turning on a garden hose, only to find that the fur and skull bones of a rat come out, or dream of pools of water in which drowned children float.

At such a time, we seem to be reduced to a body that drifts around, mere matter being bathed in the waters of death. No volitional movement is happening, there is nothing for us to do— naked, we endure, we undergo. The paradigm for our surrender to the night occurs not in the mind but in the physical body—when we are sick, when we are dying, and perhaps, for women, when giving birth. At such times there is no graceful way to maneuver the ship of awareness, for we are in the keep of forces larger than ourselves and we live or die at their behest. This surrender seems to us to be a kind of death.

For all its difficulty, we have to trust this lowering of our awareness as, eventually, we will have to surrender to the body's journey into its actual, physical death. In our descent it helps if we take toward our own suffering the attitude we might have sitting with someone during their last hours. A dying person may hallucinate, grow demented, be unable to move or speak, be in a coma. Sitting with someone in such a condition, trust is all we have. We do not trust that there will be a happy ending but that this dark moment is itself life and holds its own reasons.

When we listen very closely, there is some Ur-awareness to connect with, even in a coma. There is always a breathing rhythm, always the particular quality of mind evoked in us by the person we sit with, the particular images that visit us, different from the quality and images evoked by any other person. In the midst of neurological shipwreck, there is a tiny stirring. Keeping company with death, we stretch our capacity to honor all the parts of life, and learn that even the unendurable can be endured.

Our dreams of broken bodies and the intense interest we take in stories of loss and mortality tell us that even death *is* a something: to witness it is simply one of our tasks as creatures. Entering our own time of descent, we undergo what we may have only had sympathy with before. Then it is the business of the world to hold us, for we cannot hold ourselves.

The Dark Foundations, the Body

> ... *Now that my ladder's gone,*
> *I must lie down where all the ladders start,*
> *In the foul rag-and-bone shop of the heart.*
>   W. B. YEATS

The bottom of night has such a thick, dense quality that the alchemists saw it in terms of matter rather than process. They called it the *prima materia* because for them it seemed to be the first, gross aspect of life—unrefined, unredeemed by any admixture of spirit, and yet a kind of foundation for all that follows, for all wisdom and art.

When we reach this stage, things have solidified as much as they are going to. This bottom-substance is neutral and impersonal, but at first we experience it as repulsive and alien—foundations are indifferent to niceties. Its heaviness and lack of form make it difficult to work with. The ground of night doesn't have a direct voice and speaks in symptoms and pathology, including what we cannot bear about ourselves, asking us to acknowledge the despised and the dangerous as our own.

And the more of such resistance and pain we bring to the work, the more thorough our darkening, the better, provided we come through it. Alchemical authors emphasize the importance of beginning with the right material, which differs from alchemist to alchemist and is typically bizarre—the feces of a dog and the pus of suppurating wounds are recommended. In our inner lives these basic ingredients of the dark might be grief, rage, incompetence, helplessness, shame. In the same way, in the tale of Sleeping Beauty, the evil sprite must be invited to the naming ceremony—to the beginning of life—or she will curse the child newly born. Dark ingredients might include a terrible symptom, such as an ungovernable sexual compulsion, a violent rage, a drug addiction, or a curious symptom, like cross-dressing. Whatever is despised and given no place becomes itself the source of beauty yet to be born.

The basic stuff of matter is so opposite to spirit that this opposition comes to constitute relationship. Here is a woman's dream of what is found when we touch the bottom of the descent. The dream fragment links her inner situation to one of the great ancient stories, the descent of spirit into matter.

> I am at the foot of the stairs. At my feet I find a crumpled-up bag, and dump out the contents. A dead crow spills out. It didn't die of natural causes. Its body has been flailed about violently.

This image has the flavor of gnostic legends, in which the soul descends out of Heaven and becomes twisted and imprisoned in matter. The dream crow is a creature fallen from air and light. The carrion eater has become carrion; its feathers are dark and its life gone. There is nothing more useless or more entirely material than a dead crow—it is not even food.

Yet, as we continue to be immersed in night, and the obstinacy of the ground grows more evident and undeniable, it loses its repulsive quality. Sometimes the foundation may appear as something so small, neglected, and insignificant that it is not disgusting or frightening—it is barely noticeable. Once, in a then fairly new Melanesian nation, an Englishwoman founded an institute where she taught local artists. One began by bringing carefully copied cartoons to her—advertisements he'd seen on the streets. This was his only idea of what she could mean by art—otherwise he was utterly lost. She almost despaired. But one day, in the bottom corner of a drawing, she saw a tiny black squiggle. He ventured that it was a spider. This small dark bug was the first thing of his own that he had offered, and she asked him for more of that. It was the crucial moment. Before, nothing of himself had been worth bringing to the work and so nothing was yet alive. The next squiggle was bigger. He began to draw and paint the things around him—people and helicopters and dogs—and eventually his overspilling vision would carry him into a new life as an artist, and international renown. That first squiggle had no particular shape to it and hardly any substance, yet it formed the basic ground of his work.

Reaching the soul's own material is an achievement. When we begin the work by beginning to fall, we have little awareness of the foundation. It is bedrock, and we must be stripped down before we can arrive at it.

When the foundation appears in a neutral, unremarkable form, the purification is nearly complete. A spiritual teacher had a dream about such a moment of bare, solid simplicity.

> All that is in the dream is a black stone, like night without stars. It fills my awareness. It is the only thing.

When we do not bring our emotions to it, the basic stuff we depend on is undifferentiated and nondescript. But its appearance marks an important moment. That rock is the source. Stones compose the cathedral of Chartres and a worker's cottage, the walls of Machu Picchu and a kitchen floor. Only if we come to the foundation does our surrender matter—we have found something to build on. As Gary Snyder says,

> No one loves rock,
> yet we are here.

When the basic substance appears as a dead or mutilated animal, as we saw earlier in the dream of the dead crow, we have come nearer to the possibility of transformation. A woman had lost her way and begun to fall through her life. The beliefs that had once guided her, her strategies for living, were now under intense pressure. She had a dream in which mutilation and nourishment were combined.

> It is night in my dream. People are gathered around the pieces of a dismembered black cow.

This image shows the secret affinity between night and the spirit entering the work. The cow, unlike the crow, is an image of the world of matter that we can work with—fertile, nourishing, fragmented, lying prone, beneath all thought—and so the people gather around it. Buddhists describe a storehouse consciousness, a compendium and infinite junk shop of the mind, holding everything that we have forgotten, everything that even our ancestors have forgotten—the sight of mammoths beside glaciers, the Devonian ocean that runs in our blood, the material in our cells that doesn't have a voice. Since we are not using our own efforts, and yet something maintains life, we are at the irreducible core. We are able to embrace the difficult thing. The black cow rests in that storehouse, beneath awareness and decoration. Cut into pieces the cow is useful: it can fertilize the fields, its hide can make a jacket or shoes, and we can eat it as we eat the body of god in the Catholic communion. The death of the black cow makes life possible.

Compassion at Midnight

When it shows itself, the primal material doesn't look like the main attraction. In our dreams, there is stone. In the spiritual life, there is a parched desert or a cliff face before us, blocking the way. This basic material manifests also as the ants at a picnic, as a beggar in an overcoat outside a café. The beggar's hair is matted, his eyes are wild, and he smells. He wants food, he wants us to share our last crust of bread—acknowledging our kinship with him and with everything humble and rejected. How we treat him will be the turning point of our life. If we accept him, we accept our own darkness and, at the same time, gather him into human company.

At such a moment, in the old myths, the beggar turns into a god. And to what will we be entitled if we feed the disguised god? We will never run out of the blessings of Heaven. And what are they? Oh, nothing in particular—olive oil, grapes, a seat at the table, a bed, the sight of children running from us into windy weather—the true color of our own lives made visible to us, the riches of soul. Here is a woman's dream in which the primal stuff, just by entering awareness, asks for our kindness.

> I have a child—a baby who is black, neglected, unknown. I don't recognize this child at all. I didn't realize that I had another child. I'm very confused at first. But then I realize that I can nurse the infant, whether or not I recognize it. I can look after her.

In this dream the infant is like the baby Jesus—a hiding place of the spirit, the divine in disguise. When we see the foundation as an infant, we are beginning to love it, and with love, compassion appears in the midst of darkness, compassion that will eventually help us find our way into life again. The next story takes this theme a little farther.

A woman once told her lover that she had cancer when she did not. This action is so far outside of common sense, it is recognizable as an act from down inside the descent. Still, she explained herself to herself by remembering that her father had beaten her while telling her, "If you don't lie, I won't hit you"—but he hit her anyway. She began to lie as a protest, and mostly she would lie that she was sick. She knew that with both her lover and her father, she wanted to evoke pity and sympathy—the kindness that links people—and to find relief from the intrinsic suffering of her life. Then one night she had a dream:

> I am in the house where I grew up. My parents look tired and sad. The house needs cleaning. I have an impulse to clean it for them so that they will find themselves in a clean, sunny house and be happy. I start cleaning.

This dream is not interested in whether the woman is in a tangle with her lover or even whether she is lonely. Instead it shows a softening toward the icons of her inner life: her dream parents have become small and human, and compassion has appeared as a natural force. The dreamer feels concern for others, an impulse to deal with the dirt and stains of life. Perhaps the new direction is not here yet, but a gate has opened. To have compassion for our parents is to have compassion for our own history, and in turn to have compassion for their history, to let sunlight into the terrors of the ancient past, which are always so near. And now that she can feel for her parents' plight, it is not such a large step to acceptance of herself, of the cruelties done to her, and of her own failings. She does not need to steal a trickle of sympathy from a tired source— she is dreaming the cleansing water into being.

Compassion is a gift that appears without being called. The traditional Buddhist name for the one who has compassion is the *Bodhisattva*, the one who lives for the benefit of all other beings. Even after enlightenment, the Bodhisattva remains with others in the realm of birth and death and sorrow, because she serves the light at the center of things. This theme appears naturally when we are at the bottom of life—we may discover in ourselves the qualities of the Bodhisattva even, or especially, when we feel most lost. Here is the dream of a young woman who works with patients who have terminal illnesses.

> I have just found out I have stomach cancer. A horrible feeling of loss just consumes me. I realize I'm losing my future, my marriage plans, the children who can't be born now, my career. All the things I haven't lived and known. I ask my friends and no one can help me. Then I'm in a mall and there is a woman who has late-stage stomach cancer. They are changing her diaper right there on the ground in front of everybody. She is allowed no dignity. I realize that this will also happen to me. I call my doctor and he says that no one outside will be able to help me. I will have to find what I need inside. I wake feeling disappointed, afraid, and alone.

This is a dream of empathy, of the ways we infuse each other with our feelings and our human plight. The dreamer has entered the situation of the patients she sees every day, and her distance, her preserving separation from others, has collapsed. She is no longer innocent, no longer of a species different from the dying—she too is breaking open, and, in the end, will not even have her modesty and the protection of her clothes. The good we do has its costs, and here we see what this woman has paid, and the beauty of what she has paid. Other people will not live her life for her; now she will suffer it and enjoy it herself.

In the pit of deepest night, the figure of the pietà bides with us. This maternal endurance and reverie denies time, death, and the obvious truth that life is broken; it appears through the women bathing and perfuming the dead Jesus, through the women in a trailer home massaging the body of a dead boy so they can bend the limbs and clean and dress him. Nothing is being made here, but love is being maintained and that is enough; it will have to be enough. From this compassion out of the bottom of Hell, everything else will be born.

Empathy is an act of imagination—to participate with another person in her life is to make a connection not possible in the night of despair. We imagine our way out of the dark. But when we are in the dark, any act of will or effort is beyond us. So compassion, this poor, small first piece of the imagined world, like life itself, is born out of nothingness and is beyond anything we intend or deserve.

Coleridge records the moment of change and its involuntary grace in his poem "The Rime of the Ancient Mariner." The mariner's descent has been particularly devastating: he has killed the albatross, the crew of his ship has died cursing him, and now he languishes, adrift at sea, alone, skeletal, tormented by thirst and remorse. He tries to pray but cannot. Water snakes appear, emblems of the corruption introduced into the natural world by his crime. But still they are life: they play on the ocean, going about their ways, oblivious to him. And the mere sight of them transforms their desolate witness:

> Oh happy living things! no tongue
> Their beauty might declare:
> A spring of love gushed from my heart,
> And I blessed them unaware:

The mariner's delight and fellow feeling—arising spontaneously—breaks the spell. But his obligation does not stop at that moment. He is given an ongoing and unique character task—telling his story to strangers. This is the beginning of the path that in the East is called the Bodhisattva way. The actions of such a person are no longer selfish, but undertaken for the sake of the eternal itself. Compassion, stirring, has freed him from his stagnation and he must now touch the souls of others.

Caring for Night and Its People

Caring for the night is a strategy that we come to by hard roads. For Dante, the landscape at the bottom of Hell suffers from insufficient features: there is no song, no creature, no warmth. All is ice, frozen and without movement. In the inner life, there is no seeing, no perception, no capacity for attention. By caring for night and the life made during darkness, we claim those pieces of ourselves that seem irredeemably stuck in matter, the deficiencies and flaws of everything neglected, deficient, stubborn, resistant to illumination, unable to rise. We look for dawn in an inward and downward chasm where we must learn sweetness with our pains, acknowledging that sorrow, like joy, has its own integrity and landscape. The griefs of life beg attention; they are orphans, they want to be loved, they hold out their small hands, which grow larger and more substantial when we take them.

The body of Jesus, broken on the cross, offers an image of the primal matter. It is the body of a criminal abandoned by his intimates, tortured and given a slow, shameful death. Since the situation is beyond human repair, the corpse is taken down and given to the rock of the tomb where eternity may do what it will. And women come to bathe and anoint the body: their care for the broken corpse softens the dark a little, and after three days of inert death, a door opens. When the new time appears, we find that the dark does not disappear all at once and forever. Compassion wakes us to our labors. Like Dante with his guide, we leave Hell to enter Purgatory, the place where burdens are taken on for the sake of love.

Chapter 5

Climbing into the Light

Love's Tasks

Like the stars over dark fields, love is the gift of the eternal forces. We do not know why it appears; it is just the song the universe sings to itself. And, like other beauties, it is a demanding guest. As soon as love arrives, we have to serve it—we were naked and now must put on clothes and work.

There is a happiness in taking on the tasks that lead us out of the darkness. Work gives us a place in the world—a place the child finds coming behind the grown-ups with a little broom in the kitchen, or holding back the flap of hide as the kangaroo is skinned beside the fire. In Dante's Purgatory, as opposed to his Hell, the souls carry their suffering gladly, knowing that it purifies them and so brings them closer to God. This is the time-honored attitude for spiritual labors, in which joy comes from a lack of self-ishness. Our pleasure is to carry the right burden, and this is the result of the change that came over us in the darkness, when we had no strength or conscious wish, and love came to pull us through.

In such a way a parent sits up with a child in fever, bathing her forehead. The parent may be dog-tired and will have to work tomorrow, and the night watch is long and frightening, but sleep is not his first desire. The child vomits on him and he does not mind—he is happy to be worried, to smell the smells of sickness, to have a child who is alive and needs to be washed. These labors themselves make him a parent, giving him a life beyond himself.

Such unselfishness can appear in very hard times. One of my childhood neighbors had been on the Burma Road—a name that sent a shiver through all who heard it. During the Second World War, the Japanese had used captured troops as slaves to build a route through the tropical forests of Southeast Asia. The men were starved, beaten, and killed at whim. My neighbor was set to break-ing rock, where he fell in with a group of Cornish coal miners. It is not clear how these men had been chosen for such work—whether they got there the way Brer Rabbit found his way into the briar patch, whether it was a random assignment, or whether for some other reason. But the miners saved my neighbor's life—they taught him how to hear the sound of a hammer. Tap, tap, tap, tap, they would go all day, using as little force as possible, listening to the different voices—the hollow booms, the dull notes—mapping fault lines in the stone. At evening, he said, the Cornishmen would strike the rock a couple of times in the right place and it would shatter. In this way they appeared to be working continuously and also produced a small quota of broken stone—not exhausting themselves, not attracting notice, serving their captors very, very slowly. Their patience and their intent listening preserved them and they shared what they knew: attention and love were intertwined.

Sorting the Grains, Working Our Way

As we emerge from night we separate ourselves from its confused mass, tap by tap. In Genesis, order appears with the division of chaos into day and night. Sky and earth are distinguished, and everything else follows—grass, stars, creatures, and the drama of awareness. Spirit enlivens the thickness of matter, shapes separate out, form appears. At this moment of our journey, when we are just beginning the first ascent, the creation also happens within us.

In many ancient stories the ascent begins with an impossible task of sorting or distinguishing. In the tale of Cupid and Psyche— a soap opera of classical times—Apuleius gives an account of the heroine's emergence out of darkness through various labors. It is a story that contains many elements of the inner journey—a fall from innocence, two descents, tasks undertaken during the night, including a visit to the underworld, help from unexpected sources, and finally an ascent followed by a union in marriage.

Psyche (usually translated as "Soul") was the youngest of three sisters, and so lovely that people began to attend on her rather than on the shrines of Venus. The Goddess of Love, angered, asked her son, Cupid, to make the human girl fall in love with some dreadful outcast with no prospects. Meanwhile, since no one had the courage to propose to such a beauty, Psyche was lonely and miserable and began to hate her own charms. Her parents consulted an oracle, who advised them to prepare her for a wedding with a vile winged monster terrifying even to the gods. Psyche's innocence seemed to have attracted catastrophe, and she herself, as a dutiful daughter, insisted on following the oracle. Her parents dressed her in mourning and left her to await her grim bridegroom at the top of a cliff.

In a surprising development, a zephyr wafted her down to flowering meadows, where she fell asleep. After resting, she awoke and entered a splendid palace, where she was served by invisible hands and guided by invisible voices. In the dark of the night, her husband came. He treated her sweetly, but there was something odd about him, for he forbade her to see him. Still, one becomes accustomed to the strange, and life went along, until, one day, after becoming pregnant, Psyche wanted to reassure her family of her survival.

Though her husband advised against it, she brought her sisters into the palace and gave them gifts. But the sisters were spiteful. Envying her fortune, they convinced the girl to light a lamp and kill her lover while he slept, for he was, they said, a monster who devoured pregnant women. Holding a knife aloft, Psyche lit the lamp and saw, asleep in his splendor, Cupid, the God of Love himself—indeed, a terrifying winged monster, though very beautiful.

Half swooning, she let a drop of hot oil from the lamp spill onto that compelling shoulder; he awoke and fled.

Psyche then wandered about looking for her husband. By playing upon their greed she brought destruction on her sisters. But she could find no protector, so her only choice was to cast herself upon the cold mercy of her mother-in-law. Venus beat the girl and gave her four tasks.

The first task was to sort out a huge mound of seeds—of wheat, barley, millet, lentils, beans, poppy, and vetch. The labor was impossible, but ants helped her and eventually the seeds were divided into their kinds.

Psyche's second labor was to fetch golden wool from deadly, magical sheep. She was about to kill herself in despair when a humble and friendly reed told her to wait till late afternoon when the sheep rest and she could gather the wool from briars.

The third labor was to fetch water from the inaccessible source of the river Styx, which was guarded by dragons. An eagle came to her aid, filling the jar for her.

The fourth labor was to enter the underworld with a box and ask its queen for some of her beauty to bring back to Venus. This time she received advice from a kindly tower, which she had climbed, again in despair, in order to fling herself to her destruction. The tower instructed her to refuse any requests for help on her journey, no matter how deserving or pitiable the supplicant might seem to be. Further, in the palace of the underworld, she must refuse an offered banquet and a comfortable chair, but sit on the ground and eat only a piece of bread. Psyche followed this advice and obtained the box. Since the Goddess of Love is the source of beauty, we ought to be suspicious if she asks us to obtain some for her, but, on the way back from the underworld, Psyche could not resist opening the box. A deadly sleep overtook her and she swooned, but lovesick Love, her stricken husband, had by then recuperated enough to fly out and retrieve her. In the end, Cupid persuades the ruler of the gods to make the marriage official, and Psyche and Cupid live as immortals together in the heavens.

We who journey are Psyche, the ingenue. We fall, we always do; we are left forlorn. But Psyche's first fall is not sufficient; it has created the conditions for awareness, but awareness is still missing. The night continues to darken and another descent occurs when the lamp oil spills onto Cupid's skin. Psyche must match, harmonize with, the austerity of the night for, even in the underworld palace, she is not yet at the bottom and must stoop further, until she sits on the floor itself, eating only bread.

Venus hates Psyche for all the usual mother-in-law reasons, but underlying this cause for her ordeal is a deeper truth. In order to know union we must have separation: we have to be someone apart from others before we can be loved and join them in the daylight. As she sorts the grains, Psyche is no longer defined only by her relationship with her lover, Cupid. She is discovering her own capacity to do, to make, to be aware.

The individual life appears as we rise from our dark bed. We have seen how one woman found compassion when she dreamed of cleaning her parents' house. Like Psyche she is no longer identified with those parents, and, in performing tasks for them, she makes her own life. Her fate, her inner experience, her suffering have become separate from theirs. She can feel *for* them because she is *not* them, and this separation is the beginning of freedom. Job, too, has the benefit of a God separate from himself, with whom he can quarrel. Awareness, then, is not a passive receptivity but an achievement, a consequence of many tasks. At the beginning of the ascent we have to earn our awareness and actively intend to develop it.

In her journey toward the basic, low condition of matter, Psyche receives help unsought, even from inanimate things. She knows an upwelling of empathy, of participation, a sense of affinity with reeds and towers and birds. And what of the ants, who help her to sort the grains? I fancy they are spirit in disguise, so easy to overlook in the odd forms it takes, hiding in the ignored bits of life, sustaining the girl when she is beyond other help.

Cutting Off the Mind Road

During her travels in the underworld, Psyche must refuse to help those who plead with her—if she joined them in their world, it would claim her and she would never win freedom. Refusing the world's call and clamor is essential to certain stages of the path. Refusing what is asked or offered opens us to the visits of the spirit, and it refreshes the soul by hindering its activity, letting it lie fallow with the black earth, straining for nothing, avoiding nothing.

When the eccentric Zen teacher Ikkyu, alleged to be an illegitimate son of the emperor, was asked, "What is the essence of

Zen?" he replied, "Attention, attention, attention." Now, on our journey, as the first ascent begins, we turn upwards once more, toward the light of our innocence. Developing our attention is the first labor of this turning, and the precondition for other labors. There are many ways in which attention can be gathered—fishing, breaking stones, playing violin, performing surgery, talking on the phone—but the core of them all is the spiritual work of meditation or prayer, service to the eternal emperor whose legitimate child we all are.

Meditation does not itself accomplish the tasks of life but provides spaciousness, bringing the great background near, so that whatever we do, rising in the quiet, has force and beauty. In meditation, we take time, sit down, watch, while the silence accumulates—which is how the spirit gathers to a vessel the soul has prepared. This silence is the transformation of death's quiet stillness, which is so near and overpowering when we are sunk in matter at the foot of the journey. Spiritual silence can appear in the midst of any concentrated activity. As we ascend, it will be ever more with us—piercing everyday events and staining us to the core—but it is best cultivated through meditation, since meditation has no purpose.

At first, the practice of "Attention, attention, attention" is a struggle. We learn how much complicity we have had with the dark. We turn toward stillness, but our thoughts and feelings are in the way. Themselves life, they come so fast and thick that they crowd out life. We see how we have let our senses grow thin, diminished, pallid. I remember taking up meditation in a formal way when I found I was unable to watch a sunset. Looking out over the interminable blue and gold interior of Queensland with the last parrots swooping home, I could assess, comment, and have opinions, but was unable to let the landscape and the vanishing light simply act upon me; my disorderly awareness deprived me in the midst of plenty.

If we look inside at such a moment, we find that we are still trapped in the descent, the tumble of consciousness—thoughts, emotions, and sensations running one upon another. In fact, an extraordinary disorder is usually going on—a jumble of plans, griefs, obsessions, joys, comparisons, amusement, serenity. None of them is wrong in itself, yet the accumulation makes us suffer. As much as our actions, our thoughts and feelings weigh us down. An old Chinese teacher, Wumen Huaikai, put it like this:

> It is imperative to cut off the mind road. If you do not cut off the mind road, you will be a ghost, clinging to the grass.

Meditation, then, is a fasting of the heart in which, for a time, we do not go with our wanting and our fear. We cease to attach so strongly to the things of our lives. This is not because they lack worth, but because, when we are full of them, there is too little of us; we cannot discriminate between things, or love them enough.

Life is the gift that we do not deserve or earn. It is one of the paradoxes of the spirit that to receive this gift we have to practice awareness. On occasion it is enough just to open ourselves to what comes; but at some point we have to master the techniques of the trade. In this, the inner work is not different from studying the piano. The first task in meditation is to focus on, give all our concentration to, the breath. We attend, for the duration of the meditation period, only to the breath, in an exercise equivalent to practicing a Bach prelude.

We do not go *with* the material that rises in awareness. If we are happy, we return to the breath; if we are sad, we return to the breath; if we are bored and thoroughly sick of meditation, we return to the breath. If we feel hungry, if we have a clever thought, if we find a new plan, still we return to the breath. If we are filled with peace and serenity, and sure that we are making progress, again we return our attention to the breath.

When we develop our attention in such a primeval way, we are like Psyche refusing a comfortable chair and a banquet. We know that we are still close to the dark where it is good to be simple, to eat plain food; we are not yet ready for a feast. So we attend and then again we attend. Inside and outside, the world comes and goes, while the breath—life's basic and natural movement—remains.

As inner distractions diminish, we see that our attention has been too narrow, has taken too small a view of the possibilities of being human. Our plans and fears and hopes consume our energy but are often a kind of dreaming apart from their objects—we want this, we can't stand that, we are confused about something else, and such buffeting is just a kind of opera that is always going on inside. We discover empirically that our part in this opera is to suffer.

> The fault, dear Brutus, is not in our stars,
> But in ourselves. . . .

It becomes clear that grabbing things makes us want more things; hating people brings about more hatred; ambivalence, too, perpetuates itself. We can test this by observation, and find that when we let all this activity come to rest, we are the inheritors of a natural joy. We do not miss our former habits of mind. They seem to belong to another, ghostly existence—insubstantial, unfree, blown hither and thither. It is a relief to see what we see and hear what we hear and not wish anything in the world to be different, "not to think / Of any misery in the sound of the wind, / In the sound of a few leaves," as Wallace Stevens wrote.

When the heart fasts and we don't pursue the world, the world begins to come to us. Just as restraint prepared Psyche for her true marriage, an inner austerity prepares us for the dizzying riches of life, which we cannot yet quite know. A woman had a dream that parallels Psyche's refusal to be distracted, refusal to turn away from life, even in an apparently good cause:

> I am entering a ballroom, about to step onto the dance floor,
> when a woman tries to catch my attention. She looks wan
> and helpless—full of need. I pause for a moment, drawn to
> her, but then I turn away, toward the ballroom, and sweep
> out into the dance.

Some things we have loved will die—in this dream, the woman who does not enter the dance disappears from the dreamer's regard, just as those to whom Psyche turns a deaf ear fall away behind her as she travels. The soul learns that everything has its time and that when something dies it makes room for the new.

Attention feeds the new life. For the time that we meditate we are free even of our own desires. Our caring is not for the things in the mind but for the ground of the mind itself. We want nothing, avoid nothing. We do not clear up confusion, we argue with no one in our heads, we are not right or wrong; neither are we guilty or successful. We are like Walt Whitman's animals: "Not one is respectable or unhappy over the whole earth."

In another dream, the same dreamer witnesses one of the great stories of our century:

> On the horizon a vast line of refugees is passing. They are
> hungry and cold. I come up to one who has only one leg. I
> am terribly concerned for him, and can barely bring myself
> to face his suffering. But when I approach, he is not con-
> cerned. He is smoking happily, and laughing and joking
> with the people around him.

Such a dream does not say that we should ignore refugees, who carry for us not only their own meaning, but also memories of our ancestors and their wanderings. Instead, the dream seems to criticize an inner attitude in which we can be so involved in suffering that we ignore the lazy, sunlit forces of growth. In a gesture of solidarity, Simone Weil starved herself to death in London during the Second World War by deciding to limit herself to the rations that the captive populace of Paris was officially allowed. But in France, as one who was in Paris observed, there was the black market, and people used trickery of all kinds to survive.

Weil's suffering was a movement into the world of spirit, a

surrender of this world to the evil that is so apparent in it. We honor such a gesture—we cannot say it is wrong. It is like that of the Albigensians who were burned alive by the soldiers of the Catholic Church in Provence in the thirteenth century. They too were gnostics who thought of the world as primarily evil. Their community produced fine poets and singers and treated women with respect, yet they died because they would not accommodate to the impurity of life. Such issues rise and fall, down through the centuries. But this dreaming woman is making a choice different from Simone Weil's. She has discovered that life can have a visible happiness, she is taking Psyche's route into the love of *this* world.

Psyche's tasks are clearly impossible, and when we begin meditation it is the same. When I first began to sit in meditation, I just didn't have the concentration. I could sit down, but I couldn't track my mind well or focus on my breathing. One of the standard methods of concentration on the breath is to focus on our out-breaths. Being aware of two or three in a row was an achievement for me. So I decided to sit quietly for half an hour twice a day without worrying about the quality of what happened. This moment was like the one in which Psyche surrenders and waits, helpless, in the room with the pile of grain too large for her to sort. It took about four years of this before my meditation became at all steady or clear, but that four years was a precious time, when the surging of my outer and inner lives gradually became more shapely. With this method, we don't address directly everything we want changed; instead we wait with the dilemma that life has given us, and let the world take care of itself for a while.

Talking Back to Night

What is life but to fight
The trolls in heart and mind?
Henrik Ibsen

Beginner's luck occurs in spiritual work, and quite soon we come upon moments of effortlessness and peace. But this is a promise of things to come; for now, it doesn't last. Then the method we are following asks to be described in tougher images. On the altar of a Zen temple there is often a figure of Manjusri, holding a sword and a book—like a Jesuit. The book contains wisdom; the sword kills the old habits of heart, the unconsciousness fused with the dark matter. The presence of the sword tells us that our ascent will also mean effort and sacrifice.

The dark clings like lice in a schoolboy's hair—it grows fond; it doesn't want to leave our warm bodies; it hinders and assaults us. Just when we are starting to relax, night will reassert itself. One way it returns is through our painful moods. Perhaps these moods are a visitation from the soul, which has begun to feel neglected; perhaps they are just a feature of the landscape, like the frightening paths that Psyche must walk. We can't do much about them, just wield the sword and return to the road. By struggling with them we build our confidence and our sense of worthiness. Even if we are again overcome by the darkness, if we have offered a sincere struggle, then we are fortified, we are stronger when the wheel turns upwards once more.

Moods have an inhuman quality. In old tales they appear as foxes, faeries, trolls, and angels, whose energy and purposes are disproportionate to our realm and condition. If we are too hospitable to them, even the most apparently beneficent can destroy us. So there is a time to resist a mood, breaking off the train of emotions because it is overwhelming us and we have become identified with it.

In meditation this is the time of fierceness and endurance. If we are meditating and we hate it, fine, we keep meditating. If we get a great new idea, we keep meditating. Our great new ideas take us away from the simple tasks at the beginning of the ascent. The moment Prince Hal becomes Henry V, he leaves Falstaff, the drunken companion of his roaring days, without a backward glance. In the same way the sword of attention separates us from the false friends of our unconscious life.

The problem with a mood is not in the stuff that fills it—the stories and flavors and history—but in its intrinsic simplicity and wrongness. A mood is like a demon, wrong in itself. Moods are too high and too low. In the first condition we are carried up as if by a yellow balloon; a voice tells us that we are fascinating and successful. We are slow to tire of that voice, yet listening to it, even for a little while, we are weakened, made open to comparisons and envy.

In the second condition, the balloon is suddenly in shreds and we plunge without hope of a soft landing. We make a kind of assault on ourselves, in which we have too large an estimation of our personal faults. We hear ourselves saying that we have done wrong and will never be able to set it right, we will never be happy or deserving of love, we will never succeed at the most important projects. This moment is not the same as the time of utter darkness when we are in the pit of despair, fogged in, incapable of opinions or plans. Rather, this is an attack that happens on the way out of darkest night.

Moods come with grand words and general ideas, but as intelligences they are less than we are, prone to think in terms of the best and the worst and to make unnecessary comparisons that squeeze out life. At sunset there is no best or worst. The fishing fleet is black against the horizon, the surf goes *thump* and its white streamers drift up the cliffs, the fog bank swallows the sun before the colors can stain the sky, the cold rushes across our cheeks, and we remember a moment long ago, when we were happy and cold, and the surf goes *thump* again, and pelicans, freighters of the bird world and also a kind of fleet, dive into the darkening waters where the herring have shoaled. A mood can only remove us from the evening's sharpness. It is common to think of moods and despairs as genuinely earned and part of our personality, but that is their deception—they are propaganda from the Ministry of Despair and the Bureau of Grandiosity. When Psyche turns away from them, when the meditation continues to plod humbly along, these moods, like other old advertisements, wither and grow stale.

In our task of attention we acknowledge that we are not innocent, that the darkness is also our own—that we have a taste for night, for failure and need. It is this we must confront in ourselves. It becomes an act of will to sit silently and be aware, or even to get out of bed in the morning.

Liberation from the Lord of Death

The power to separate from the night grows in us as we grow more familiar with its citizens and devices. Here is a dream of a woman who imagines the relationship with the dark as a kind of bad love affair from which she has to free herself. She is ascending but feels the downward tug.

> I was in a room and heard screaming outside. I went to the window and saw a man dragging a woman along the street. The woman was tied up in an elaborate harness like a strait-jacket. I went outside and yelled at the man to let her go. He did.

The dream shows Hades and his queen in a domestic moment. Even in the most serene of lives, many things oppress us—self-criticism, the opinions of others, the general suffering within and around us—and this woman is becoming conscious that inner events have real effects. The struggle to enter the next stage of her life has begun. If the dream ended here it would illustrate the process of separation nicely, but the dream goes on:

> Then the man asked me to get into the harness and I agreed because I felt so powerful. I then persuaded the man, of his own free will, to release me.

In a complicating twist the dreamer takes on the harness herself. This is worrying—like the moment Psyche opens the box of deadly sleep on the way back to Venus, or the moment Orpheus turns back at the gates of the netherworld and loses Eurydice, the beloved. Psyche is always attracted to the warm dark that embraces life, destroys life, and makes life possible once more; she will always open the box that should be left closed. While we long to ascend, we are also pulled down, willing to return with the soul to her confining palace, content to stretch out in the dark while her unseen lover comes and goes. In that narrowness she floats, trusting, among invisibles, without choice or anguish. This downward pull is so strong that we have to return again and again to the same labors, which is why the interior work sometimes seems endless.

Yet there is another deep truth that appears when the dreamer steps into the harness, the girl opens the box. Psyche and the dreamer are both making their own lives, and this is the last task of Purgatory. As we rise, even what seems to be error serves us. Both women triumph by transgression: Psyche disobeys her mother-in-law, and the dreamer disobeys common sense. They act against our expectation, and this makes them unique. The soul is released from striving, and progresses by moving *into* the darkness, and this movement leads to freedom. We continue to rise and the unexpected becomes natural.

Chapter 6

The First Silence in the World

Innocence Again Draws Near

Spring comes with its flowers, autumn with the moon,
summer with breezes, winter with snow;
when useless things don't stick in the mind,
that is your best season.

WUMEN HUAIKAI

As we persevere in the tasks of the upward road, we discover that stopping the mind road is not an addition of effort, not a struggle to stay with the breath, but a release of the burdens we carry—our pride, our anxious attachment to even trivial outcomes, our ancient griefs, our efforts to be good. Psyche falls into slumber and then other forces can aid her. Even at the very beginning of meditation, as we struggle to uncoil the tendrils of night, we get a glimpse of a place we are not yet ready to inhabit—a field of silence and the freshness of new-fallen snow. The virtuous pains of Purgatory are subsiding, innocence again draws near, and the engines of eternity bear us up. The experience of meditation can now be described not in terms of what we hold on to—the breath, though we do hold on—but in terms of what holds on to us—the primeval silence. In this fashion our meditation is like Psyche's sleep.

The ancient basis of spiritual practice is always stillness and silence. We may sit under a tree, cross-legged in a quiet room, or by the fire; the important thing is that we turn toward an intense inwardness. There, silence comes to us out of the dawn of the world—from the earliest band gathered on the sandstone cliffs, looking for the sun to rise; from the hunter waiting in the spinifex grass for the kangaroo, holding the spear out of sight, in his toes.

We are at the waterhole at dawn. The beasts arrive and drink and leave, yet we remain. Thoughts, memories, sorrows, excitements—they rise and have their time and fall away. We sink deeper into the silence until it becomes its own desire and fulfillment. We yearn to immerse ourselves, to touch this ground every day. Even our longing, though, is just something in the mind, a barrier to the truest silence and the barest perception. When we do not cling even to spiritual things, we find that we have fallen into the mystery beneath the beneath of life, underneath even the dark matter, beyond knowing and not knowing—and at this moment life returns to us without its veils. Devoted attention sets us in relation to the source. Everything is born out of the silence—grass, rivers, stars, children, animals, and love.

Naming the Animals

From the point of view of the great silence, the labor of sorting the grains, which seemed before so hard, becomes easy and graceful: all being comes to help us. We return to a time utterly fresh—we name the animals in the first garden. Whatever is newly born needs a name, and now that we are more and more welcomed by the silence, naming becomes our job—we have to notice, to bless with attention the beasts before us, both the rough and the smooth.

To name is to bring an attitude of wonder to the work of sorting, and even to the work of dealing with difficult states of mind. When we can name what is happening to us, we are no longer wholly identified with it and have begun to separate from the grasping dark. If what we feel is known and named to be a tiger, then the whole world is not tiger. We can divide the compulsion and the image, the action and the emotion. There is a landscape through which we move, trees casting their own stripes on the forest floor, places where tiger is not.

At dawn, the world appears on the shores of the vast ocean. Out of the mist come crocodiles, wombats, Land Rovers, and courts of justice. Separation gives us being and world. Being accumulates in each of the things that appear from the waters. And *there* on the shore, we who are ourselves barely dry, we who are also pieces of the original stuff, fall in love with other pieces, saying, with primordial delight, "woman," "man," "apple."

Everything has to be welcomed and acknowledged and with this movement soul too becomes intertwined with our ascent.

When we give names we devise an intimate link with what is named; we incur obligations that serve to establish us more steadfastly in the daylight realm. Adam named the animals on parade before him, and the biologist in the highlands of Papua New Guinea says to herself, "This, not this," again and again, until she comes up with a name for the blue butterfly, as large as her hand, adrift before her. To name is to offer a piece of ourselves to the world.

And something, some portion of soul, has endured through loss and descent and crosses over with us to the other side. Night itself has generated love, with its images. When we sort and name them we begin to attach to the images, and to distort them in an assimilation crucial to life. During the sack of Troy, Virgil imagines Aeneas, the Trojan hero, escaping from the burning city with his father on his back. In turn, the father carries the little images of the gods that are a kind of seed to found the new city that will someday become Rome. The images, like names, give continuity and shape to what we discover. The soul goes secretly to work, bringing depth and richness to the strange newness that we enter as we escape the dark.

Later what has been separated out may come to seem too solid and will need to be dissolved again in a union of spirit and soul. But for now, this is just what we need: the delicious predictability and otherness of things, the beginning of consciousness.

The Second Surrender

As we persevere in the work of the spirit we find that we undertake a second, voluntary surrender, parallel to the despair of the previous descent. In the first case, we surrendered because we had no choice. Now, as we rise, we surrender by letting go of what weighs us down and binds us to the night. After this there will not be much question as to whether we shall continue on our journey. We become ascetic in a voluptuous, lolling sort of fashion: we give up whatever is in the way, recognizing that restraint provides the conditions for sweetness. This is not austerity for its own sake. In the monastery of the heart, spareness is our luxury and welcomes life in.

There is a story of a scholar who came to study with a Zen teacher. The scholar knew exactly how meditation could benefit him and was eager to begin. The teacher was courteous and offered tea. The scholar tried to be patient while the water heated. Eventually the teacher began to serve the tea. But when the cup was full, he did not stop pouring, and the tea ran down the sides of the cup onto the table and off the side of table onto the expensive tatami mat floor. The scholar, aghast, said, "Stop! Stop! The cup is full." The teacher pointed out that the mind, too, cannot take in something new until it has been emptied. This story illustrates the value of having gone through the darkness of descent—sorrow empties the cup.

Spiritual work is erratic until we decide to keep doing it no matter what, to make the disciplines of attention an ordinary part of life. Surrender also acknowledges the power of this good work, accepting that it goes on even when the results are not obvious. This is a consoling realization, as will be seen from another story by the woman who, in her earlier dream, stepped onto the dance floor.

> Recently, before a seven-day retreat, I ran into a younger man who often had painful meditation experiences and wished him "a good retreat." "I know all your retreats are wonderful," he said, and I thought, "No, it's just that the horrible ones have become wonderful, too."

The Tears of the Way

When we surrender, the soul begins to help with the spiritual project. Soul doesn't seem to travel any faster than a horse, so it makes the spirit wait until it can catch up. A sudden regression can occur just when we feel that we are doing very well. Such hesitation allows us to catch our breath and pat our pockets, to make sure we have included the whole of us before we step through into the new life. This is like the moment when Psyche, having completed almost every task required for her freedom, opens the box she is carrying back from the underworld and is assailed by deadly sleep. At such a time, we can't see the bottom of our emotions or where they will lead. Each new degree of nakedness seems to be absolutely required of us. We need the patience to bless even our weakness, this odd weakness that seems to come not when we are helpless, as it does in the darkest night, but when we are full of strength and rising.

Such a lapse into inexplicable waiting happened for a woman who had achieved considerable spiritual force. She was in a retreat, had attained the steadiness and confidence to press on, and felt a confidence and clarity begin to emerge—nothing spectacular, but a growing assurance of her welcome on earth. Then suddenly, she seemed defeated by an unexpected grief. As the retreat continued, she just watched her life move before her, and she wept, day after day, until the weeping itself began to change.

I had been meditating deeply and begun to feel that, through this practice, I was finding my balance for the first time. I became flooded by memories of my father and of the pain I had suffered from his absences and from being handed around to foster homes, neglected and disregarded. I had thought that I was opening up and then suddenly this, this thick, personal material seized me. I was totally caught up. I wept and wept. Everything I saw seemed a fresh occasion for tears. As I watched for several days, my mood began to change and the tears became more impersonal, causeless—the tears of being moved by life. I was seized by a tenderness, especially for unseen, neglected, and abandoned things—a particular shade of blue in the sky at dawn, the bones of mice dropped by owls.

These later tears are the tears of initiation. Tears, like blood, are life's water, a fluid anointing the time, dissolving obstacles and hardness of heart. They unbind us, translate us to ourselves, are the medium in which we move between one way of being and

another. We cannot say that they have any other, particular meaning. And while tears of this kind are not the same as the tears of
grief, they take the place that grief used to occupy: something
large is turning over in the inner life, and this means great changes
are on the way. We shall not be who we were, and some acknowledgment of what is being left behind must be made.

Our most sincere effort can convey us only as far as the frac-
turing of certainty. Then we enter the straits of passage, and, weeping, say good-bye—to our prejudices and petty wants and also to
the control of our fate. We are taken up into largeness. This happened to me during a month-long retreat, when I began to open in
spite of, or perhaps because of, strong inner turmoil.

It was one of my first intensive retreats, led by a jolly Tibetan
lama, who, with his gloomy assistant, also Tibetan, visited Australia. They made up for their inexperience with Westerners by
their enthusiasm, generosity, and very traditional Asian teachings.
The gloomy teacher, whom I didn't much like, would drone on
each long summer afternoon, and I would wriggle like a school-
child. I began to suspect that my irritation was rather shallow, not
really the point. One day as I was listening and meditating, not
doing anything special, I began to weep. This was quite involuntary. Weeping was not, at that time, in my repertoire, yet there was
no impulse to dam the flow. In that moment I felt that I was on the
shores of Galilee, hearing Jesus speak, and understood that all the
great wisdom comes from the same source.

With my amazement, compassion awoke in me. It didn't matter if the teacher didn't understand Westerners, if he wasn't such a

great teacher, if I wasn't much of a student, if my character provided infertile ground. I knew that I could not judge these things
accurately; at that moment it was not important to consider them.
I was weeping the tears of the way.

Lightness

While soul is grounded and moist and has roots, spirit seems to
want to rise—into air, to white mountains, to the sky, and to pan-
oramic views of mortal life. So our climb toward the light, while it
is interlaced with moments of soul, belongs mainly to the tran-
scendent realm of the spirit.

Nirvana, the traditional Sanskrit term for being awake, refers
to the snuffing out of a lamp and, by extension, the extinction of
all desire and attachment to life. This aspect of the Eastern tradition reflects a stance that puts spirit at the center. When Buddhists
take initiation names referring to stones, snow, and nothingness,
or Christians long to imitate Christ, to live without stain, to be
celibate, to do only the works of God, they follow this impulse.
Spirit consoles and heals through its impersonal force. There is
lots of space but no furniture in its living room. The attitude is
perennial: in many traditions, orthodox spiritual fantasies are
about translucence, stillness, equanimity, refuge from the flux.
The yearning for transcendence entails moving away from the
body, refusing the condition in which we are, as Yeats so emphat-
ically put it, "fastened to a dying animal." Even in the pagan
world, no one was allowed to die or be born on the island of

Delos—the shrine there was not to be tainted by our blood, our mortality, our life.

My early Tibetan teachers had a good cop, bad cop routine. The laughing one would evoke the joy of life and then leave us to the mercies of his more junior assistant, who pointed out the inevitability of suffering and taught us to imagine our own deaths— the farewell to life, the disintegration of the body, the awareness that remained. It seems a natural process, now that I have seen more death, but at the time I remember haggling about what I would give up first, as if I would have a choice. Much of the struggle of accepting death seemed to go on unconsciously and was revealed in the difficulty everybody had in concentrating, the facility with which we fell asleep during the interminable lectures, the frequency with which we stole off to start love affairs or to look for chocolate. That retreat was a painful struggle—but I learned to ignore aches, sorrow, plans, memories, spiritual ambition, and other usual entertainments and to discover meditations composed of nothing but clear space. The radiance of the jolly lama began to make sense, because his buoyant spirit was founded on an acceptance of the descent of suffering and an objective knowledge of the mind. And this is the strategy of the spirit—to release our tight hold on the foreground of life and turn toward the vast background that we call God. We are grateful, then, for the distances and space that compose the spirit.

There are many forms of this filmy evanescence, this lightness of the spirit. Some emergency room physicians use black humor to maintain sanity and even empathy without identifying with each agony wheeled through the doors. And a dying man may not be interested in his pains, may take great delight in the sight of a rose, of a tired nurse brushing back her hair, may understand that this moment in the oncology ward is also eternal life. His spiritual practice is just to listen and watch and breathe.

The Immortality of Childhood

Tears cleanse us and pull the present moment around us. Then the spirit takes over again and meditation retrieves the lost, endless afternoon of childhood—innocence in its positive aspect. At the moment the newborn infant is thrown into the human realm of wailing and hunger and soft skin, her eyes seem to carry a memory of the unclouded spaces from which she has so recently arrived. It is as if a vast being peered out through the tiny form, and, for a little while, we can peer back in the other direction and see eternity. Youthful, pristine, unfurrowed by experience, the spirit has an affinity with the child. We remember all our lives the things we met as children—the kitchen smell of cooking oil, rosemary, and thyme, the early winter darkness folding about our shoulders. Such things make the world for us, they carry the taste of life itself, the threads out of which we weave our story, and the reason we came here to have a body, to dwell in houses and walk in shopping malls. As it grows, the soul will work with such ingredients and make them dense and resonant, but now they are simply clear and vivid. The Zen teacher Shunryu Suzuki made popular the notion of beginner's mind—in the beginner's mind are many possibilities, he said; in the expert's, few. Spirit has this mind of setting out. When I lift my infant daughter to see her first rose, her eyes grow wide; it is as if she falls into the expanding petals. And, as I watch her, she is my rose; I too sink into the firstness that still surrounds her.

The clear mind, then, belongs to spirit. In spirit's domain, when we taste Seville orange marmalade—so bitter and sweet—there is for that moment nothing else in the world; when we hear rain, it is the eternal rain, the rain beating on the galvanized roof of a hut in the mountains of Tasmania, the rain sliding silently off the windows of a high room in the Fairmont Hotel in San Francisco, while the traffic runs in rivers of light far below. The eternal rain is not happy or sad, it is eternal; and that, in itself, fills us with joy.

At the moment of birth, the spirit is life itself, all there is. But there is nothing to hold the experience—while soul and character may be developing moment by moment, they have not yet arrived. In our maturity, often the opposite is true: consciousness has developed, but the openness is not there. In order to grow we have had to take a particular form and forswear all others, to develop a way of loving and of fighting, a taste in music and in food. We choose without knowing where our choice will lead—we are shaped by what we seize and what we refuse. This path is human and good, but we pay for it with the loss of our original fusion with the eternal, when spirit filled the most of our days. So when spirit comes to an adult, it comes as a return and as an astonishment—impossible, beautiful, alarming, it cracks us open.

I remember as a boy standing at the side of a gorge in

Launceston, in Tasmania, watching the swift, shallow water and a girl standing in it up to her knees. Everything was settled and at peace in the sunlight. As I watched, the hills began to sing—I could hear them as an indistinct choir. Then they began to shimmer and dance. It seemed clear that we were linked—hills and humans—in a deep, objective way. And this connection made life true, and my usual fears irrelevant. My ordinary worries about love, fights, exams, and winning games, and even about the death of friends— all of these were foreground against a great background, and, at that moment of inner stillness, the background had come near.

Years later I learned that this was a common experience in the Zen tradition—to see the mountains dancing, and witness the se- cret joy at the heart of the universe. But I was not then particularly spiritual in inclination; I was a boy in high school, a football player with an interest in literature. In retrospect, it seems odd that I wasn't surprised, but I wasn't. "Ah, so it's true," I thought. "I had suspected this all along without knowing that I did." Most of us have known this kind of unsought mysticism—we are going along about our business when suddenly an angel touches us on the shoulder. We recognize that light pressure; it is as if we have been waiting for it all our lives. Sometimes a very young child will say things like "The tree is talking to me." The child is not just an an- imist, attributing her own life to everything else; she offers an un- derstanding of the communion of each thing in the universe with each other thing.

A woman tending a dying friend took a weekend off by the ocean. When she walked outside, the landscape opened up, and she saw each daisy and poppy in the field as the whole world, and she fell into them—herself dissolving into the expanse of sky and air and the flowers. The late *plein air* paintings of Monet speak to this sort of epiphany, and also Blake's lines:

> To see the World in a Grain of Sand,
> And a Heaven in a Wild Flower;
> Hold Infinity in the palm of your hand,
> And Eternity in an hour.

Hearing the voices of crickets and the pulse of the hills in this way, we know the bass note of joy underneath human misery and pleasure. We are content with our portion of the greatness of life and with our portion of its sorrow too. The mere memory of such an experience can carry us through our hardest times. After his death, his housekeeper picked up Blaise Pascal's overcoat and found it oddly heavy. Sewn into the lining were papers containing an account of his own meeting with eternity, the story of which he carried everywhere with him, next to his skin. "Tears," he wrote, "tears of joy." A good spiritual tradition offers a map through such experiences and a way to consolidate the gift, a packet to carry in our coats, its weight pulling at us slightly in the supermarket and the boardroom.

As a child I once tossed a coin off the wharf into the dark water. I can feel, still, the shudder that ran up my back as it disappeared. Now, I think of wishing wells, where money is thrown into the water as a payment that enables us to speak our dreams, and of meditation, in which whatever we clap onto is soon released and leaves no trace. I suppose the boy staring into the water was standing on the threshold of the life, so much greater than himself, that was all about him. Everything he did seemed irrevocable, and what he had sacrificed in order merely to live and to grow seemed lost forever. When I discovered meditation, it became for me a way of recovering that childhood coin.

Repetition

There are tools of transformation. The art student draws a hand, a face, the curve of a back, over and over, quickly and slowly. Gradually her consciousness changes and the hand, the act of drawing, and the person drawing become transparent; unity is restored to the world. At the moment this process is complete, the student is no longer an apprentice. Some Tibetan Buddhists undertake a foundation practice in which, among other tasks, they perform one hundred thousand elaborate prostrations, usually over several years. Now, this might seem quite useless and of no benefit to oneself or others, yet it too offers a way to enter life utterly. One lama laughed and said that the first ten thousand or so prostrations he did were not any good, so he threw them away. Then he began to do them more simply, more entirely. The days and months continued and the trees became vibrant, the eyes of the people he met grew vivid with their story.

Repetition is narrow and, if undertaken mechanically, stifles us, but it can also allow us to go deep. In meditation we repeat ourselves day after day, coming back to stillness and the breath, and again and again realize that we haven't yet experienced it completely, that it is ever more subtle. Repetition, when done right, drifts almost imperceptibly into vast, new realms, but with a slowness that allows for deepening, beauty, the appreciation of the neglected moment. It stabilizes our relation to eternity.

Any good relationship—marriage, a love affair, friendship, teacher and student—depends as well on just this sort of steady, attentive repetition. Common events, like having breakfast together, accumulate significance. Repetition teaches us that the things we do are not confined to their practical value. Bowing, or even lifting a fork from a plate, makes us aware that simple acts share a common timelessness with the sound of the spring wind and of the branches banging on the gutters.

The Next Step

Repetition may seem a succession of small moments, modest and uneventful. Yet repetition has also a certain cunning: it forces us to bide a while. The passage of time so gained alters us—we learn the small arts of attention and how to love the domestic moments between the big moments; we are soothed. But the road of repetition does not just make us calmer, more docile to ourselves. The step-by-step rhythm opens out, in time, to a surprise.

For repetition makes us vulnerable to the apparently random epiphanies that occur even if we have no interest in spirit. The boy immersed in his life stands amazed on the side of the gorge while the hills dance, the woman steps out of doors and dissolves into a field of flowers. Such events appear in our lives as gifts, apparently random. If spiritual openings are accidents, as a number of teachers have pointed out, then the spiritual work of meditation makes us accident-prone, susceptible to the imagination of eternity, the wit of God.

In matters of the spirit, no road is ever straight. When first we begin to open, the vastness can be frightening and so we regress, sag back into the familiar darkness, where we can be close to the earth and rest. There we abide, gathering invisible resilience, until once again the involuntary compassion appears in the midst of suffering, and we step back onto the stairs of Purgatory and the steady repetitions of spiritual work.

Just why the door within begins to open is a mystery. But if we follow a spiritual method it *does* happen; we are thrown into vastness as into a sea. Since we are each unique in what we bring, there are many different ways of being cast upon the infinite. But always we meet something greater than ourselves, beyond all we hold important. When we are utterly ready for it, this vastness is no longer frightening, but comforting. It is so far from the common experiences of life that it seems to hold nothing at all, to be a great nothing, and that is the Buddhist name for it—emptiness.

The Consolations of Emptiness

For the listener, who listens in the snow,
And, nothing himself, beholds
Nothing that is not there and the nothing that is.
WALLACE STEVENS

Body and mind fallen away, the fallen away body and mind
DŌGEN KIGEN

The stillness of meditation can become so profound that it takes us back, before our personal history, before our ancestors made their long journeys across continents and through caves, and into the dream that made the world. We find ourselves in vast space. All about there is nothing—just as if we stepped out onto the tundra in winter. Our equanimity is large, impersonal, unruffled. The bottom drops out of our lives and the transparence of the world is revealed.

This time of clarity is an echo of the moment of thick darkness when we confronted the inertia of matter. That was the first stripping away. But this time, when we are stripped down, it is a release. We have acquired strength and can now examine what is happening rather than just suffer it. We see that the physicality of matter is not the very foundation of the universe. Beneath it is what gave it birth—the mystery underlying even darkness—from which the earth itself with its mountains, oceans, buildings, animals, people, and clouds is born. The traditional Buddhist name for this mystery is *Sunyata*, usually translated as "emptiness"—

but emptiness is a feeble term for a realm so noble, vibrant, and clear.

Here is innocence in its deepest aspect—without stain or disturbance. It is a kind of solution in which everything is dissolved. The solid melts away; our small schemes are surrendered, and the universe takes its Sabbath rest. Our sorrow and our struggle both vanish into nothing. All is still and full of strength, like Wordsworth's London when he saw it from Westminster Bridge at dawn:

> This City now doth, like a garment, wear
> The beauty of the morning; silent, bare. . . .

In the silent realm, our customary language breaks down and metaphors, which abhor a vacuum, gather around. The emptiness is the host of which we are every moment the guest. It has been called the sword that kills our delusions, the cloudless sky, a jade palace stretching for a thousand miles, the arctic snow fields. In one tradition, the experience of emptiness is called the realization of no-self, while in another tradition it is known as the discovery of our true self. Our small lives have opened into the infinite and into belonging. It is a great release to know down to our toes that we are each of us waves of the ocean and that each wave is entirely ocean and can never be other than ocean. Our small lives have also ceased to be so emphatic, firm, and rooted as they were. If we are ocean we are also wave—passing, insubstantial, foamy dreams.

The empty realm is not a place we may live in, but if we want freedom, we must pass through it. It is the gate of spiritual initiation, the destination to which our sincerity, our foolishness, our suffering, our meditation and prayer have led us. Even the most commonplace things seem dreamlike and magical. An old Chinese poem gives us this description.

> In a well that has not been dug,
> Water from no source is rippling.
> Someone with no shadow or form
> is drawing that water.

Here, the common life is still common but it rests recognizably on a mystery.

If we stumble upon this place early in our work, before we are ready, it may have a desolate air. If we are not ready, if we have not yet turned our lives toward attention, if we are unused to the way meditation and prayer loosen the hold of our routines upon us, we can become afraid. Some people feel the boundaries slipping away and fear madness. What is happening is that our views of the world no longer cohere. So a certain psychic robustness is necessary to accept this experience, to allow ourselves to enter it fully.

A woman walked in to see her teacher, said, "Everything is gone, there's nothing left," and burst into tears of loneliness and fear. She was in no danger, but felt that she was. Her fear meant that she was not quite ready; her quickness had outstripped her strength. Whenever we are blocked in this way we just need to wait—to take breath, to gather steadiness until, again, the silence appears, space becomes visible, and we can allow it, accept it, witness it underlying all that we are. Then the stillness is experienced as calm. The thoughts in the mind stop. Nothing is necessary or urgent. Here is another woman's description of such a moment:

It is as if I am sitting in a cathedral on Easter Saturday. The struggle and tears are over. The doors of the empty tabernacle are flung open. It is a quiet waiting. There are no trumpets. Nothing has been reborn yet.

The vision of emptiness is not just the awareness of the flimsy, unravelling thread of life. It is more a glimpse into the dream through which we move. We see there is nothing to stand on. Because there is nothing to stand on, because we have lost all guides, an eerie beauty seeps in. When everything is taken away, the remnant is eternity, the emperor worth conversing with. It seems then that we are always one with eternity, for in our current form we are its thoughts and feelings.

One man fell into the empty kingdom when he went with some friends on an afternoon hike. He was not prepared and had no idea what was happening, so the opening seemed to him a kind of a crisis.

I was on Mount Tamalpais when it came over me that I wasn't there. It shocked me. I had no training, no preparation. I was jumping around on Mount Tamalpais, hitting my body, trying to convince myself that I am me. Something in me was saying, "You are not you." I wasn't there. I looked at the redwood trees—heard the siren going off at the bottom of the hill. I was saying my full name. "I am myself," I said. And some voice inside was reassuring me, saying, "This is okay, it's okay, my friend." This part of me was just peaceful—everything was all right.

The realization of emptiness replaces endurance as the healer of the night. We ask ourselves, who is it who suffers? Who is it who exists? And we cannot find the bottom of ourselves. We cannot find anything to stand on. Instead of being devastating, this clarity is refreshing. It becomes clear how much egoism there is in all despair, which fails to realize both the seriousness and the absurdity of our situation.

Some people who feel desolate inside are attracted to the notion of the emptiness of things because it seems to mirror their lack of inner organization. But true emptiness is not psychopathology. The nothingness at the bottom of the world is the creative emptiness of the divine—it is full of possibility and has an impersonal flavor. We may use poetic phrases to describe this realm, but it is not something we make up.

Even within a meditation retreat, the experience of things falling away can be surprising. Perhaps it is something for which we can never be entirely prepared—one minute we are immersed in suffering, the next moment a kind of grace strikes us like the red light of morning. One woman was meditating cross-legged when her knees began to hurt badly. She didn't give up, though; she sat very still and focused her awareness. Along with other things in her mind, the pain surged and receded and surged again. Then suddenly the pain lifted completely. Her mind too seemed to lift and expand. She said:

> The walls in my mind seem to have disappeared. It is like looking out over an ocean that goes on forever. A quiet ocean. All the way to the horizon, everything is just space and more space. There is no container, no border, no skin.

Such emptiness is the taste of eternal life. It is not that it satis-
fies our small, self-centered wishes—when confronted with eternity, we no longer care about such longings. But to have tasted it
even briefly is enormously sustaining. It sweetens our human loneliness. We know that we too participate in the world's dream, that
we too have a true part in the life of the universe.

Everyone who pursues the meditation path with diligence
eventually comes to know this spaciousness. It operates in difficult
times and ordinary times and good times: it is not limited. Here is
a story of how that peace can be present in the darkest of moments.

One night in the city, a man heard cries and ran to help. A
young friend, almost a brother, had been shot and lay bleeding on
the gray pavement. When everything that could be done was
done, and the ambulance called, the group of friends who had run
to the scene stood there, just waiting, keeping company with the
now dead young man and his world. The man looked at the street,
the purple blood, the lights. To wait is good. It gives time for the
world to turn and something else to come along. But this waiting
extended and spread out. Time had stopped. There was nothing to
do in the whole universe. Everything was simple, complete, still;
each thing had equal weight. The man felt himself utterly present.
He was not at odds with his aspirations and his feelings. His grief
and his love of life were not contradictory. There was no gap between him and death and his companions and the tears and the
street. And his grief formed itself into a question: "Why can't we
see this all the time? Why can't we live like this?"

This incomprehensible peace under duress is the taste of the empty world. At such a moment there is nothing to be done and this nothing has to be enough. The intimate attention of the man and his companions is their blessing on their friend, so irrecoverable, so newly dead.

Our boundless awareness seems as if it will last forever, but it does not stay. It is itself still a kind of waiting, a sparse, pristine consciousness, the deep form of the sleep of nothingness into which Psyche falls along the road of the dead. In the inner life, this emptiness is not the journey's end. During the winter we can trust that spring is also there, under the ground, waiting. Small tokens do come—a swelling daffodil, a few bees stumbling among them. We can see emptiness still, underneath our every turn, the great engine of life, producing all that we are. But just as Psyche is raised up for her wedding day, we are drawn away into a human brightness. We jump into the void with only our courage and the beauty of the world to sustain us.

Chapter 7

The Enlightenment of Rivers and Grass

The Longed-For Catastrophe

Within nothingness, there is a road.
Wumen Huaikai

Winter has stripped us down, we leap into nothingness and the spring comes crashing out—a benign catastrophe in which the beauty of the world assails us and is victorious. The organizing constraint of the personality, which psychologists call the ego, falls away, and we soar, or spread out, or are overwhelmed, according to our abilities and to the rigor of our preparation.

The experience of the mystery and emptiness of life is a disturbing gift—we are in the predicament of Alice who, in order to get anywhere in the Garden of Live Flowers, must head in the opposite direction. We are consoled *because* we lose ourselves, along with our common burdens. In this, awakening is near to love, and to that deep suffering that can disclose an unforeseen sweetness. The wreck of the old life opens the new. Even when the wreckage has been dire, our pains themselves can become transformed: they are taken up into the vivid story of the new life, and in this talismanic guise, will never be forgotten.

We wake because we have been discontented with the cramped, ghostly air of the lives we have been given. We want something greater than ourselves—we want to be loyal to life's promise. We have arrived at the edge of spring by stripping ourselves down, like El Greco's saints, who have shed many colors and qualities so that their bodies and even the cliffs of Toledo have elongated, stretching to be closer to Heaven.

This work of simplification has been in part painful and in part exhilarating. Our weaknesses and delusions, after all, give us shape, so when in spiritual work we lose our talent for being comforted by outer things—the gleam of a new car, the admiration of our peers—we grow more bare, more passionately poor, and that is how we arrive, shivering and naked, at the winter place. But spiritual preparation has also given us the capacity to be terrified without flinching. Then we *do* feel something letting go. "I am pecking from inside, won't you peck from the outside?" a Chinese pilgrim asked his teacher a thousand years ago. Every experience we have is an example of the universe pecking, apparently randomly, from without—an opportunity to wake up. Another traditional story shows a series of these pecks.

Yuanwu Kechin was proud of his spiritual knowledge but was

rebuffed by his teacher, who said that his understanding was not yet valuable, that he was still blown about by the wind. Yuanwu left in a huff, but as he walked out, the teacher said, "Remember me when you are sick with fever." Years passed. Indeed, one day Yuanwu did become seriously ill, and when he recovered, he came back to his old mentor, who quoted a popular song:

> She calls to her serving girl, "Little Jade,"
> Not because she wants something,
> But just so her lover will hear her voice.

When the teacher said, "That is very like Zen," Yuanwu awakened. The ancient human disaffection with creation, the sense of being outside the garden of life, dissolved for him, and everywhere around he heard the world calling, just for him. But we ask ourselves, at what moment did the world peck from the outside? When his teacher confronted him, when he caught a fever, when he heard an old song? It seems that our lives are full of these pecks.

Catalysts

For spring to occur, something needs to appear—a blossom breaking out on a black branch, a daffodil opening its yellow throat. Enlightenment, too, enters our lives with a catalyzing event. Eternity appears through the world of form, the evanescent and potent realm of our actual lives. It comes always in embodiment, as a particular thing that appears hugely in the vast space that meditation has uncovered. An object, a movement of the mind—our mind or the great mind—appears and takes up all the view, as his teacher's words did for Yuanwu. A particular thing—the thing that stands for world—reaches out and seizes us, as Cupid flew down and picked up the prostrate Psyche after she had opened the treacherous box of sleep. Here is a story of this seizing—a story in which the catalyst is splendidly commonplace. The account is by a woman who had started to "crack open," as she called it, at the same time as she happened to become physically ill.

> I couldn't drive myself and I asked to be driven to the Zen Center. I looked into the eyes of one of the priests there and I fell into his eyes. It seemed as if an eggshell was cracking around me. Then we were driving home and I was in the passenger seat, listening to the radio. And—this was fantastic—an ad for an old TV melodrama, like *Dynasty*, came on. A woman's voice said, "If I can't have him, Jessica, nobody can!" and then there were gunshots, "Bang! Bang! Bang! Bang!" That was it for me. The freeway turned into a river of light. Everything was a wave coming up out of that light—each individual thing. I saw that all being is the ocean of that light. Or it is as if there is a great hand and all things are the fingers of that hand. Everything was lit from within and glowing. The light was thick and viscous. The air was thick with it. It was an ugly part of town and a stupid ad. But the ugliness fell away, and everything—freeway and warehouses, trees and sky—was all equally beautiful. It changed how I saw Fairfax Avenue forever.

In the end, the long-sought change comes involuntarily, as an intrusion of eternity. Our hope and labor alone cannot make it happen, though hope and labor prepare us. Awakening requires also the cooperation of the world. The freeway, the grubby neighborhood—we must have for our spiritual company all the ordinary shapes of life.

Here is another account of the way the commonplace can seize us, this time coming to a man alone in a room, not doing anything in particular.

> I was sitting in my apartment and looking at the radio dial when I merged with it. That's not quite the way to put it. It wasn't that I fell into the thing—it came to me, it became me. I saw the way everything arises each second from its source, all of the universe coming into being, and linked to everything else.

When we experience any one thing to the depths of our being, then the universe opens itself to us. We can see who we are and what our part is in the drama. Koun Yamada, the modern Japanese teacher, liked to say that enlightenment is the dropping away of the self in the act of uniting with something. This intense focus is a mark that at such a moment, while soul is indeed nearby, spirit now predominates. When we fall into one object we are confined severely in its single, narrow passage from which we emerge into vastness.

One Thing Before the Eyes

The catalyst awakens us; instantly it fills our sight. When we have emptied our minds and hearts of passing things, we have emptied life entirely—this taste is the spirit's flavorless flavor, like snow melting in the mouth. Then we find that we have merely become impartial, and life returns to us, the more breathtaking since less of our small selves is painted upon it. The woman mentioned above, who had fallen into grieving for her childhood, her father, life, described the effects of her initiatory weeping. Her tears had, in Blake's phrase, cleansed the doors of her perception, and after they had finished, she began to walk about the retreat grounds, looking at the reeds and the bay.

> I was picking up rubbish on the trails. I don't know where the tears went. They were just gone. But I could see this rubbish as having its own value, like everything else on earth. I found a flattened beer can and it was the most beautiful thing. I took it into an interview with my teacher and put it on the altar, because it belonged there.

For her, at that moment, the discarded metal was life itself, the goal of her journey achieved. What she had longed for was available all along, contained in even the most crumpled, dusty form. In such an encounter, the dark, disordered stuff of matter has become sacred. It is as if a summer-green pear tree appeared in a level snow field. Whatever we meet is wholly remarkable and absorbing. The light, faint touch of emptiness appears as the boundlessness within which all objects and emotions are afloat. The world seems remarkably uncluttered, like a Vermeer in which the jumble of sustaining things—the platters and jugs and brushes that would have surrounded a Dutch person of his time—is reduced to one or two. The balance scale a woman holds up, the pearl in a girl's ear, her gaze resting upon ours as she turns—all seem to step forward, to approach us. There is space for the objects of our regard to rise and endure in the moment.

A Chinese Zen student of some thousand years ago described how we persevere in the journey until we see the clarity of the eternal world as vividly as if what is before us were the one thing. He tells how he studied alongside Guishan, one of the great teachers of the Tong dynasty's golden age.

> I lived with Guishan more than thirty years. I ate Guishan's food, I shat Guishan's shit, but I did not study Guishan's Zen. All I did was look after an ox. If he got off the road, I dragged him back; if he trampled the grain in others' fields, I trained him by flogging him with a whip. For a long time how pitiful he was, at the mercy of everyone's words! Now he has changed into the white ox on the bare ground, and always stays in front of my face. All day long he clearly reveals himself. Even if I chase him he doesn't go away.
>
> CHANGQING DA'AN

The most vivid experiences are always the consequence of others less vivid, of a readiness that has accumulated. But at the moment of vividness, the pains of the journey seem small; the one thing before us is all that has ever existed. The white ox of heart and mind just as they are, of the world just as it is, stands before us on the plowed earth. We see our own nature and the universe's nature as precisely the same. This seeing dazzles us, shows us our home, and gives us joy.

A Peach Blossom or Two

One spring day twelve hundred years ago, an old Chinese master called Lingyun Zhiqin was walking along. He had meditated for a long time and grown absorbed in that life. Summers of heat and dust, freezing winters had passed over him. Then he rounded a bend and was amazed by peach blossoms on the opposite hill. The shock of that tree in flower awakened him. It was the custom to write a verse on such an occasion and his words went:

> For thirty years I sought a master swordsman.
> How many times the leaves fell, and the branches
> burst into bud!
> But from the moment I saw the peach blossoms,
> I have had no doubts.

In any initiation, sacrifice plays a part; a sharp blade is needed to amputate the old life. Here, the sword was peach blossoms. The shock of their color and flutter cleared up Lingyun's uncertainty. His spring occurred during the ninth century, in China. That branch was still in bloom in the fourteenth century, in Japan, when a teacher called Keizan Jokin wrote,

> The village peach trees
> were not aware of their own crimson,
> yet still they freed Lingyun
> from all his doubts.

These blossoms stick to the memory as to our hair, to the wet sleeves of our coats on a blustering day. They are entirely themselves, fragile and brave. And they make the world so transparent about us that we join them, we become them. The blossoms are something small that allows us to enter the present moment without regret. The stark, absolute nature of the catalyst—the one complete thing in the world—opens outward so that the city street with its buildings, people, and cars spills its brightness all about. The spirit, pure and austere, begins to meet the soul so full of multiplicity.

A man falls in love with a woman not just because of her beauty or learning but because of the tenderness she gives to frivolous things—the slight rapacity with which she leans toward a cup of coffee, the curve of her arm holding the *New York Times*. He finds this a relief, he *recognizes* the gesture. He has fallen in love with the intelligence of her soul and of the world that imagines such a being, the world that endows such a small moment with an enduring glow. The old Chinese sage too has fallen in love, been led simultaneously further into the world and beyond it. The tree overtook him and the moment is still bright today, as the plum trees are opening into rain showers outside my window in northern California.

People have come to awakening through hearing a flute on a beach during a war, through breaking a leg by catching it in an iron gate. Still, Lingyun's peach blossoms are especially endearing for the bright, cloudy associations around them. They come so briefly after the underworld time of winter, out of a stillness in which not much seems to be happening. They hold also the excitement and frailty of being human, and the bright largesse of certain moments—the red of a glass of wine, the dancer's many-folded skirt, the space between hay hill and sky at twilight, the intricate, cantata-like progression of sorrow and laughter.

When we look into our true experience of the world, we always come to a strange twoness. As humans we are more fragile than we can bear to know, buffeted by war and earthquake and also by the endless risings from within, by obsessions and longings, fear and anger. Yet at the same time, eternity presses itself upon us continually: it is near the way the hillside we stand on is near—forgotten, enormous, the source of nourishment and rest, thrusting up the grass spears where we lie down at ease. Both truths are always applicable: spirit brings its everlasting radiance, and soul helps us to receive the spirit's overwhelming gift.

Any authentic opening of mind embraces the greatness and smallness of who we are. Old Lingyun met the flowers with his whole being and this encounter was so strong that we can enter it still; image and poem carry it down to us, and when we see it ablaze across the valley, no time has passed. Yet this experience happens entirely within the everyday. I round a corner and the norwesterly winds fling a few wet petals onto my chest. I get a cold and sneeze.

We awaken to the extraordinary in our lives—and the common flow does not change. We have our rhythm; we work, eat, drink, and talk together into the night. The catalyst becomes the only thing in the world, blossom or radio dial. Then we recollect the eternal, the hillside we stand upon and the source of blossoms and radio dials and cars and showers of rain among sun shafts. In our awakening, when the spirit is to the fore, what overtakes us, what shakes us till we wake, is stark, stark—pristine as a beech forest—and unarguably, blessedly real. Seen in the soul's light, eternity is voluptuous and an endless fusion with delight.

Narcissus and Daffodils Spill from Her Arms

So, with just one thing appearing in the desolate space of the universe, spring comes. But spring is not just one thing. The white ox is the spirit's animal; for the soul, spring appears as the goddess of forms and multiplicity—as Botticelli's Primavera, who has flowers in her hair and on her dress, and is herself a kind of gorgeous bloom. Spring comes with a tumble of colors. Its joy is not the only thing, but it is one of the great things—to have a human form and to know utter happiness. Our joy is unsummoned and comes out of the plainness of the empty universe. It seems impossible that there could ever be anything at all, any form, any movement, and then, suddenly, flowers burst and buds burst, clouds scud and birds hurry with twigs. At last we are at home in this flutter and activity—an ascending song—a life without intermediate veils. The soul inhales the ticklish air. The overwhelming riches of the spring may lead some people to reflect whether winter, in its simplicity, might not have been less confusing. But we have no choice. Once we have abandoned the spacious equanimity of winter, we are flung into the world of intense particulars—each exact and brilliant.

Joy is a forceful argument, and in any event, we cannot go back to our old house, which seems so cramped and dark now, and its furniture like the trophies of childhood, with the gold-toned coating half rubbed off. It is such a relief to be free, to love what is before us, to welcome life without reservation. It is said that after his own enlightenment, Koun Yamada went to an interview with Hakuun Yasutani, and could not speak. He collapsed into his teacher's lap, sobbing with joy. Yasutani patted him on the back, saying, "Yes, yes, I know."

Ordinariness

Awakening rearranges our perspective so that we see the great background of which we are a part. In fact it is nearer even than that, we find that we are both the great background and the foreground that is its only expression. We see the eddies in eternity made by our hands as they go about—unbolting the black-streaked valve cover on an engine, lifting a vine tendril full of grapes.

This clarity of view is a feature even stronger than joy. The white ox stands on the bare ground in simplicity, without motives. Everything is clear in the vertical light of noon, unshadowed, undoubtable. We understand that our true nature has been always visible but that we received its blessings without seeing their source.

Clarity reveals ordinariness. When everything else has been taken away, what is natural remains. The bent-eared doe, the power pole, the man leaning on the open door of his truck to cough, appear in their primeval force, as if nothing had existed before. Here is the voice of a woman suddenly struck by the freshness and modesty of the common world.

I was sitting waiting for an interview, not really knowing what I was going to say; in my head, I had no idea about what was going to happen next, and I was just staring straight ahead at the wall. Suddenly I realized that the wall perfectly met the floor. Precisely! It was just so obvious. At that moment everything was good.

The ghost gum's leaf is pale green and the mare's tail is smoky white in the blue sky. At night, the nesting wagtail calls and the koala coughs, invisible in the branches. Everything is just as it is, and this exactness, we feel, is the greatest of blessings.

The Mountains Dancing

Awakened mind is large, and has more than one mode of perception. There is also a topsy-turvy strain to enlightenment—it embraces contradictions quite as eagerly as Walt Whitman did. The core contradiction is between the forceful impression of emptiness—the feeling that there is nothing at all that has absolute existence—and the equally forceful impression of the singularity and beauty of each thing. We see that the waves are really the ocean, yet the waves persist in having shape and loveliness beyond this abstract, spiritual truth. So as we open up we will say things like "The mountains are dancing" and this discovery makes no distinction between great Annapurna and the small Green Mountains of Vermont. Zen teachers in some lineages will ask a student to "make Mount Shasta dance," asking her to live the implications of what she has found, to demonstrate where the vast spirit becomes human.

In the spirit's domain, the meanings of things are loosened—up can be down, sad can be happy. The Cubist painters brought this realization into art early in the twentieth century, breaking apart the planes of the human face and torso and reassembling them in ways both surprising and convincing. Marcel Duchamp offered another version of this revelation with his readymades, taking a common object such as a white porcelain urinal and exhibiting it as a work of art.

Everyone has her own style of dancing in the world in which the meanings are not utterly determined. A merchant of the Tong era, Pang by name, loaded his fortune and possessions into a boat, which he sank in the middle of a river—a performance piece whose subject was enlightenment. He did not simply give his things away, because he did not want to burden others with the misfortune of wealth, he said. Still he remained in the web of family and trade, travelling about with his wife and two children. Here is another story of their family style of awakening.

> Once Pang was selling baskets of bamboo. As he was coming down from a bridge, he tripped and fell. When his daughter Lingzhao saw this, immediately she ran up and flung herself on the ground beside him.
>
> "What are you doing?" he cried.
>
> "I'm helping!" she said.
>
> "Lucky no one was looking," said her father.

All this nonsense is theater, laughter, illustrating the vast *isness* of the world. But the play is also, as we see here, compassion—in its meaning of sharing suffering—and empathy with the absurd.

Years ago, during a retreat I taught in Honolulu, a loud brass band started up a couple of blocks away, perhaps at the university. This is not what people usually think of as good for contemplation, but a man dashed into an interview to say, "The drum is playing *inside* my chest. *I* am the drum." He was not deranged, he knew the difference between hallucination and reality, but his view had altered and his eyes were shining—he had stumbled into the eccentric poetry of the spirit.

Intimacy

> *When the 10,000 things advance and confirm the self,*
> *that is called enlightenment.*
> DŌGEN KIGEN

Intimacy is a modest and tender name for the connection with the spirit attained after long wandering. It conveys some of the shock, greater than sexual, of being opened and revealed to the world while the world opens and displays itself inside one's own breast. Stories filled with images of meeting have come down to us out of the mists of time, and meeting continues to mark the opening of the heart and mind today.

A woman on pilgrimage to a Buddhist site in India found the conditions there chaotic, yet through that loud, impinging life she discovered her connection with others. Here is her description of that moment.

> I experienced this union most vividly in Bodhgaya—an alive
> but very crazy place—where we were sitting in the midst of

everything. I remember the call of a woman herding her cows outside the wall of the stupa—how bright and vivid it was. That one call contained everything and was everything. There was nothing else in the universe. *Her* call was *my* call. As I sat more it expanded. People were working in the fields and there really was a feeling that *I* was working in the fields.

Enlightenment has been described as a wedding, a feast, an encounter with the teacher, recognizing your own face in an ancient mirror, opening a gate into a new world, a meeting with the ancient sages, the direct sight of God. This intimacy is not limited to the human realm—it links us with stone, leaf, ant, bird, rain, and star, and with events as well as objects. The woman continued:

> There was a rainstorm then, and I had an immense joy of *being* the rain and being the grass enjoying the rain—not thinking, just being there in the room and also being the rainstorm. Everything was in a deep communication. And yet, usually we don't stop and listen. I looked out the window and I was stunned by a red bougainvillea. "Here is the voice of God," I thought. "And we just go by it."

At such a moment, whatever we see has its own dignity, carries its meanings within and speaks to us. We see and are seen. Crows and dragonflies, wheat ears and outcrops of bare granite, share our family name. When the wind blows, it blows through us, the rain slants through our chests. There is no barrier between ourselves and what is happening—we are ourselves the mountains and the birds, and the mountains and birds themselves walk about with us and drive on the freeway.

Intimacy involves recognition. The old Chinese teachers called it meeting your original face before your grandparents were born. In the sounds and the rain we extend far beyond our bodies; we are linked in an indissoluble closeness with the planet, the stars, and each other. The universe is friend.

Such intimacy changes our lives: we see at once that awakening is not just for our small selves. Wherever we turn, each thing shines with its own light, which is our light. Human and non-human, even animate and non-animate, are included in our circle, and so we are family with the kangaroos, rivers, stars, and other people, without respect for wealth or color or any other divisions. And in the same way, each moment of life is real—standing up, sitting down, and wearing clothes have their dignity and their part in the web. We come down from the mountain vistas of the spirit to travel about in the valley among the other creatures. For the sake of what is greater than the world, we are led to immerse ourselves in the world.

Intimacy restores a human scale to the immense insight of awakening. Something delicate and subtle is involved in this. Many movements of union and separation occur in the course of our inner journey. We progress as if in one of those eighteenth-century dances—now together, now apart, while the violins continue. Each of us is a wave of the same salt sea and joined, yet we come to a tenderness for each wave, so particular and separate, so strong in its feeling for its own shape, its own offering to life. Our tenderness has no intentions toward life. It is an appreciation—both a personal feeling and a recognition of reality.

Compassion for others is born of our own experience of suffering. It first appears at midnight, when suffering has wrung the self-absorption out of us and broken down the boundaries that enclose us. Then it is a surprise, the invisible thing that joins us, at last, to human fate. We learn to love, to care for the anguish of others. Now, at noon, the situation is not desperate or shocking; nothing is forced. Hearing the news that we have the same last names as the blowing grass, the glowworms in the cave made by the roots of the upturned tree, and the galaxies living and dying in their vast cycles, compassion rises like the evening breeze, a natural feature of our inner seasons. The selfish emotions give us pain, thicken us, constrict the breathing. But our feeling for others is weightless and old; we recognize the other, our original links to all life.

Compassion carries a sense of objectivity, but its nature is to be highly particular. In this way it carries our spiritual recognition into the soul's domain of love that has a body. We feel for *this* child with a running nose, whose black hair falls into her eyes when she somersaults, for *this* cliffside where the snow gums bleed red sap on their white trunks and wombats have burrowed dim palaces in the broken rock. And the more particular it becomes, the less remote: the more it moves into love. Love comes out of the emptiness. It can't be helped. Like us, it is absurd and endures through its own fragility. Gradually love draws us into the world again.

At this stage of the journey, we value small efforts toward the good. Or to be more precise, we love the little as well as the large, no longer always certain which is which. Good deeds and kindness are simple and sustaining, like bread. It is good to love the near, sweet, and present things, pleasing to the soul—the apple fresh from the tree, the children learning to read. From there, compassion ripples outwards, to the hungry child, to the alien refugee fleeing war. The woman whose awakening occurred when she saw how exactly the wall met the floor talked later about how she had been changed.

> I feel a responsibility toward the world now, which I didn't feel in any serious way before. As a child, I would take care of myself pretty much and I had certain things I had to do— my parents told me I had to go to school, make tutus, etc., but that was about the extent of my responsibility. I wasn't conscious of what others needed. I think an enlightenment experience opens up the interconnectedness of the self with everything else. There seems to be no choice. Let me think of an example. Well, if somebody has a problem and they want to talk about it, it's my responsibility to sit there and be a listener, a committed listener to that person. Otherwise I could say, "Oh, that's your problem, too bad. I'm more concerned about my own problem." I can't ignore the fact that people are suffering any longer. I noticed they were suffering before, but now I feel I have some part in it, and an obligation.

This example is very ordinary—befitting her kindly feeling for common things. The movements of compassion can be big enough to save rain forests, but intimacy also appears in the small acts that open infinitely large doors. Modest acts of courage reverse evils before they grow great; small generosities welcome children to the world. Those who recognize their connection with others serve quietly, like members of a secret order. Then the small acts and the large coalesce. In Denmark even the king put on the yellow star to show solidarity with his persecuted Jewish citizens during the Second World War—a small act and a great one, all at once.

When a hospice worker told about the death of a patient dear to her, she began with the lighter-than-air quality of the final night.

The night she died, doves came around my house and sang. Perhaps this happens often, but I had never noticed it. I still dream of doves, white doves, and think of her dying. I don't usually admit this to people at the clinic, but when all is said and done, love is the only worthwhile force in the world. There's nothing else that really counts.

Doves belong to Aphrodite, the goddess of love, and they are also messengers of the Holy Spirit, bringing the divine into the world. In their image, soul and spirit meet. But the blessing of love also brings us close to the wound of love, for love makes us submit to the unheroic weakness of having a mortal body and, opening us to each other, makes us helpless and kind.

Knowing the intimacy of awakening, we intend to love, we intend compassion, we hold up our little light and step forward. Even a glimpse of enlightenment is a sharp brightness. We want to find out what's next, how to stain our lives with that color, to be dyed all through. And so love, with its urgency for the particular, leads us further along our road and into the world, where we are immersed again, swirled about by fog, sea mist, uncertainty. For love is where we shall end up—it is where all the stories end that end well—but first there is another road to walk, to consolidate what we have discovered, still so new and frail.

| # Mortification: The Second Descent

Tumbling Out of the Light

> *Officially, even a needle cannot enter,*
> *unofficially, you can drive a horse and cart through.*
> YANGSHAN HUIJI

Spiritual awakening brings the glory of the dawn: we are charged, brightened, elevated, and enlarged. But on returning to the everyday world, we find that much remains the same. The dishes need to be done; children want to know all about the split photon experiments, of which we ourselves continue to have a weak grasp; phone messages remain unanswered; investments must be supervised and toilet bowls scrubbed. At the same time the basic wounds of human life remain: war, famine, and human misery appear at every turn, and if anything we are even more aware of the suffering they carry.

After a great experience of opening into a new way of being and looking, our task is to embody what we have found. Awakening requires some degree of union between spirit and soul, but such experiences seem almost always to drift, to lean toward the side of spirit. Spiritual love is so full of the ideal that it must learn to embrace imperfection—to descend, to become embodied, heavy, and thick again. If there is a treasure to be found in the depths of the night, there is also a valley very near the mountains of awareness. We have to fall into the valley again, to be depressed, to suffer again, just to have life.

The light of eternity fits itself into the small physical moments that make up our lives. We have bodies, we *are* bodies. Hunger, thirst, longing, foolishness, work, failure, joy, honor and disgrace—through us spirit is entangled in fragile matter, taking its shape and height and name. There is no other vehicle.

Through the Gate

In some schools of Zen, there is a ceremony called transmission, in which a new teacher's understanding of the spiritual realm is recognized. The first time I saw such a ceremony, the new teacher was already in his sixties. The old teacher, the mentor, said, "Now your practice is beginning."

It is beginning because the way is always new. The child comes to the breakfast table with fresh sleep in her eyes, the sun rises over a landscape we have never sufficiently attended to, and the oranges laid open in quarters are the first oranges from the first orange tree, golden lamps from their green night. But there is also a more mundane sense of beginning: to understand is quick and exciting but to embody is slow and penetrating. Even the deepest experience just brings us through the gate of the new realm.

The meditation tradition has always emphasized that it is important not to cling to spiritual experience: such grasping becomes its own problem, the brightness obscuring the view. There is an old Chinese expression for this: "Gold dust is precious, but if it gets in the eyes it can cause blindness." Here, a man tells about not holding on to spiritual gold.

> I walked across a lawn with a view of the Atlantic. The grass became so green and alive—I could notice the ants moving around, and there was a dragonfly. Suddenly I didn't have any doubt. I knew that we hadn't lost anything, that the old teachers were still alive, and that they could still teach me.
>
> I asked for a meeting with my teacher. He asked me a lot of what seemed like diagnostic questions. I was confident that I had entered his world, and still am. Then I fell silent, lost in the wonder of it all. He laughed and said, "Don't worry, it will pass."

Some teachers believe that it is necessary to intervene with their students to wipe away, by humor or other means, any stain that their awakening may have left. But life will remind us of this all by itself. If the first task of the inner work is to pass through the gates of eternity, the second is to be of use, to bring something back to the world and its creatures, and this means to get involved once more in the mystery of incarnation. In Heaven, where everything is already attained, there is no growth. Only the earth holds seeds, and gravity pulls us down to the earth's dark riches.

It may seem strange that even after we know one of the triumphant achievements of consciousness we should suffer a second descent, but it is true to the poetry of the way: to its inconsistency, caprice, and beauty. The second descent is part of the long, good work. It sometimes appears as an acute crisis, during which our demons, inner and outer, return, and sometimes as a prolonged time of flatness and mundane difficulty in which our best plans are thwarted and our hopes unfulfilled. Our discoveries undergo ordeal by reality. Now we learn about the darkness that attaches to achievement and leadership, and about the strangeness, the things that arrive when we are looking the other way.

Pathologically Pure

"I am going to God and not stopping to sniff the flowers on the way," said John of the Cross, impatient for the spiritual treasure, but who is to say that God's body is not in those roadside weeds? Certain kinds of purity disregard life and seem to call us toward a second descent. On earth, spring just comes—rain, the fresh shoots, blooms in the Sonoran desert—saguaro, ocotillo, hedgehog cactus, staghorn cholla, palo verde, prickly pear holding up its yellow cups. Woodpeckers go hopping among them, the little wren chases the big woodpecker away, doves coo coo in the dust, the coyote melts into the mesquite without exerting herself. Then spring goes. Once we have experienced an awakening, we want to fill the day and night with its freshness, to live in its elation forever, but this is to ask too much; it leaves no room for living, for the fading of the flowers so that they may have seed, for the losses that educate the soul.

Many times on our journey we are tempted to identify too much with the infinite, to starve in a crystal palace. Zen teachers call this condition "the stink of Zen," recognizing that spiritual attainment creates its own problems. Beauty rises before us, as in the Navajo horse songs, while we move out toward it; if we try to make it fixed, it disappears. The high moment passes and we have to spend time with the dirt itself, the dry wash, the black road, considering that the pleasure of those pebbles might also be God's pleasure, and the weeds, the garden where God may walk at ease in the evening.

The great eighteenth-century master Hakuin Ekaku went to his teacher with his enlightenment experience nicely written down. The teacher brushed the paper aside and invited Hakuin to explain it to him directly. Hakuin said, "There is nowhere to attach arms and legs to it." The teacher twisted Hakuin's nose, saying, "Here is a place to attach arms and legs."

While Hakuin was still in his exalted state, his teacher called him a demon watching over a corpse in a coffin. Eventually Hakuin stopped holding on to the spiritual heights and told his teacher of his new understanding:

> The Master neither approved nor denied what I said but only laughed pleasantly. But from this time on he stopped calling me a "poor hole-dwelling devil."

The symptom of being caught in the empty world is that we refuse to pass lightly into the stumblings of ordinary life. We swing between Heaven and Hell, forgetting that spirituality is not about the relative merits of a particular place, even Heaven. Here is one woman's account of the problem.

> When I am in retreat, I see so clearly that I am just in the light. Other people's opinions don't matter because I am at ease with everything. The only way I know I have identified too much with the light, and somehow lost my humanity, is when I crash and the depression sets in. Then I feel so deeply unloved and intrinsically *wrong*. And I'm very reluctant to let anybody in to help me.

She is describing a classic problem of the inner work in which, identifying with the spirit, we lose our conversation with it. Other people's opinions matter very much to them, and from their point of view her ascent may feel like a barrier, or an abandonment of the human. This is why serious inner training is most rigorous in its later stages. If we try to go forever beyond the inward experience of descent we refuse our mistakes and our learning. At such a time we have fallen out of harmony with spirit and are merely asserting its privilege. We might begin to find the darkness outside and to search for heretics.

The clergy are poor at governing because they identify so strongly with the perfection of their vision that they leave no room for life. They attempt to bring the rigors appropriate to the early stages of a private, interior discipline into the public realm. In the private realm, cutting off all distractions and extraneous interests, denying personal whims and fancies, turning away from everything apart from one's own narrow path, lead to deepened attention. In public they lead to the Inquisition. And even in the private realm, in the long run, if we do not accommodate our little vices they grow large, and spill over to torment those close to us.

The spiritual vices do not live only in clerics and cults. Some of the worst tyrannies of our era can be recognized as idealistic perversions of the spirit. The Nazis wanted purity and clarity—no Jews, no gypsies, no homosexuals, no modern artists, no one crippled, no one different, and, ultimately, no one alive. The Khmer Rouge of Cambodia, in a dreadful parody of Buddhist asceticism and of Rousseau's ideal of the natural human, starved a whole people and killed anyone who had an education; anyone who knew a foreigner or had a skill, even the doctors; anyone who was not unformed, naive, and illiterate. This crime is a vice of the spirit because it attempts, terribly, to subdue life to the idea, to make a union only with the perfect, the unshaped.

One of the distinct features of Cambodia's particular terror was that tears were banned—the soul's tears that bless us and dissolve a little the harshness of fate. A survivor told how, one day at a meal, she began to weep uncontrollably for her murdered husband. The other prisoners gathered silently around her to shield her from the sight of the guards: otherwise, she too would have been killed. Under such a regime of terror, differentiation is not allowed, nor the soul's operations of separation and sorting that help us into awareness. Aristotle—saner, more human and worldly, and without any great spiritual interest—said you cannot build a city with one kind of person. You need different kinds of people to make a city.

Like a totalitarian government, spirit that is too pure will eventually fall from its own excesses. If inflation is attachment to the magnificence of the spirit, the inevitable other pole is suffering, martyrdom, and sorrow. When we have lingered too long in the realm of transcendence, it turns into its opposite, as if in obedience to an ancient law. The air goes out of the balloon, and old torments arise once more. One of the tasks of the second descent is to see that while we may have learned something real, the journey continues, and its explorations and stumblings continue too—torments belong to us still.

A Darkness Out of Time

The second descent happens at noon, when our lives appear to be going well. We seem to be doing things properly; we are not ignorant or unconscious; yet things still fall apart. And so there are two common responses to this fall, each of which becomes an obstacle in itself: one is indignation—the thought that whatever pains are happening to us shouldn't be happening—and the other is despair—the thought that this is a special fate reserved only for us. Both these reactions come from the assumption that the second descent is somehow out of time and sequence. Its unexpectedness undermines two of our most loved and durable notions: that suffering has meaning, and that we can find a path beyond it through our virtue and skill.

The second descent may stem from an outer blow or from an

inner failure of confidence. Cancer appears, houses burn down. The artist runs dry, the businesswoman picks the wrong stock. The success and delight we have been basking in end abruptly. We cannot explain it to ourselves; some pains are not deserved. We had begun to think that we were on a journey designed by an engineer, but this new element of caprice and unpredictability could only be the work of a poet whose rhymes we cannot yet make out and whose images do not seem to progress to one another. One woman's description of childbirth gives us a metaphor for the difficulty of the second descent.

> I remember in the last phase of childbirth, I felt that I gave everything I had to give, completely expending my fund of concentration, strength, and energy. My daughter was born and I lay back, exhausted, to bask in the glow. No one had told me that I still had to give birth to the placenta. It seemed like a cruel joke. The nurse began pressing down on my belly, and for a moment, I hated her. But then she said to me, "This is always the hardest part of my job." I had thought the pain was over and I had my great reward. So the second wave felt unbearable.

Further surrender is required, and we earn it with further suffering, the way Job learned that it was not his place to talk of reasons to God.

John Keats thought that there was an ongoing necessity to learn through suffering. He wrote, "Do you not see how necessary a World of Pains and troubles is to school an Intelligence and make it a soul? A place where the heart must feel and suffer in a thousand diverse ways?"

Only when we throw our hands up do we become free of fate. If we do not grasp and cling, there is nothing to fear, nothing to be taken from us, nothing we need. In the same way we might say that Job, with his final, inner surrender, became, at last, free of God.

The old Chinese had an appreciation, even a fondness, for the caprice of the inner work. One of their images is still given to meditators, some time after they have had a deep experience. It is this: "The clearly enlightened person falls into a well."

Public Mortification

In its public forms, mortification usually means a sudden plunge from the heights. In the English-speaking world, the great, terrible example of mortification is King Lear. In his age, he decided to give his kingdom away and devised a test that chose precisely the wrong people to give it to—his two daughters who were vicious flatterers triumphed over his sincere and truthful youngest daughter. Lear lost his wits, his children, his kingdom, and his life; even the weather was harsh upon his noble, feeble old head.

There is always a second descent for the illustrious. The one who had been yesterday adored is today derided; people he hardly knew, and to whom his only connection had been to perform mild favors, appear in print to declare that he has always mistreated them. Oscar Wilde stood waiting on a railway platform as he was being taken to prison. He stood in handcuffs before the gaze of those who had admired him and who now, with no significant change in his behavior, despised him. Tragedy and comedy are both made from this kind of plummet. U. S. presidents often seem to suffer in such a way. Because of his fatal passion for Vietnam, Lyndon Johnson saw his great record on civil rights obliterated and did not seek a second term. His death from a heart attack seemed to be a further withdrawal from the stings of public life. Richard Nixon's paranoia erased his achievements in China. Ronald Reagan, affable and out of touch, standard-bearer for traditional values, saw his child write a book attacking his ability as a father. Success is as dangerous as failure, as the *Tao te ching* says. The strategies by which we came to success rarely help to maintain it, and mortification teaches us that the disciplines of the inner life must continue whether we are at the heights or in the depths.

Fleeing the Body

The great public dramas of mortification are enacted within us when we make in the inner life the same mistakes the famous make in their outer sphere. The spirit tries to find its way into the world without regard for any other factors, disregarding precisely the small, temporary, physical gestures that make life amiable. Such hubris leads to the inevitable explosion of whatever has been excluded. Folktale holds this knowledge too: in the story of Sleeping Beauty, the king and queen neglect to invite a faery to their daughter's name feast. This faery puts a curse on the infant so that later she pricks her finger on a spindle and falls into continuous sleep. What is refused, returns.

In the flight toward the spirit, the body can be lost as a source of wisdom. Often a part of the path, as we have seen, involves a deliberate investigation into the body's transience and fragility. But any revulsion against the body is not useful in the long term.

Often women are asked to carry and bear the blame for what the culture has not come to terms with—the pleasure, the untidy fascination, of having a body; the fathoms and altitudes of feeling. One executive of a notable and even adventurous Western temple banned the sale, in postcard form, of paintings of Buddhist wisdom figures because they had naked breasts. Spirit does not quite accept the body; when it is too dominant, the position of the feminine declines in status. Tolstoy, eager for saintliness, leaves his wife. Somewhere at the nadir of this impulse is the world of the fanatics, where women are dragged out of cars and beaten for the crime of showing their arms.

Children may suffer too, since they are insufficiently angular for the rigors of the spirit. The care of children demands immersion in the moment and can be a form of meditation or prayer, as can cooking, gardening, or tending the sick. Spirit has a theory of liking children but a practice of making the conditions of their lives difficult; resources and time are not allocated, messes and noise are not allowed. In the realm of government, senators often like to praise Christian family values while voting to cut education funding.

Spirit is wonderful with last things—death—and first things—the mystery from which we came—but we humans are very interested in all that happens in between, in the meanwhile of a walk on the beach, reading a novel by the fire, throwing a stick for a dog, chopping garlic, of the unimportant moments that give life its true flavor and only justification. We all have an unlived side that calls sirenlike to us—clergy lust and criminals dream of being humble and pure. Watching the way spirit seems to soar and crash, I wonder if even a great force like spirit may not also long for its opposite, harbor a secret interest in plummeting, a curiosity about the earth and the body. As our inner life deepens, we don't really want to be perfect ethereal beings, beyond pleasure and pain— that sounds like the Hell of Virgil. The soaring of spirit is a fine thing; the error comes if we cling to spirit when it is time to turn down toward earthly realms, the pain of skinning our knuckles on a cold morning, the pleasure of loving and loathing.

Isis and Osiris: The Soul Works with Mortification

> *Sweet are the uses of adversity,*
> *Which, like the toad, ugly and venomous,*
> *Wears yet a precious jewel in his head.*
> SHAKESPEARE, *As You Like It*

One ancient Mediterranean story that includes both the first descent and the second is that of Isis and Osiris. Isis is married to Osiris, whose brother Set kills him. This death is the first descent, in which the force that pitches us into night is unexpected, yet already intimate with us—the brother, our other self. Set locks Osiris in a casket, which the tide carries to the base of a tamarisk tree on the Phoenician shore. The tree enfolds the coffer and, when it is later cut down to make a pillar, gives off such fragrance that Isis is led to it.

This fragrance seems to be the same fragrance that appears in tales, popular in Tibet and China, of meditation masters whose corpses give off perfume and light. Something is changed in the darkness, something is revealed as precious through all the transformations that life takes us through. In *The Tempest*, Shakespeare describes it like this:

> Full fathom five thy father lies;
> Of his bones are coral made:
> Those are pearls that were his eyes:
> Nothing of him that doth fade,
> But doth suffer a sea-change
> Into something rich and strange.

Gathering the Pieces of the Fragrant Body

Isis recovers the casket, and this is the culmination of the first descent and the ascent to awakening, which follows. The lost treasure is found again, time is suspended, betrayal and anguish have been transformed into perfume. So far so good. But Set, the shadowy force in us all, is not integrated completely by transcendence and sweet odors. The new spiritual experience will be tested. In just the same fashion, the new celebrity finds that her fame has given her quite a different set of problems, and in some sense has made life more frantic and impossible.

Set comes upon the body again, and this time does a more thorough job, dismembering his brother and scattering the pieces about the Nile delta. When we have achieved a certain level of awareness, we may feel our stings and griefs more acutely, having lost the thick skin of former ignorance. So Set brings about a second fragmentation of consciousness, a second death, a second descent. What happens next shows the way Isis works with the second descent.

The queen becomes ever more resourceful in the face of disaster. She wanders about, collecting the pieces, and wherever she finds a fragment she builds a shrine. Each fragment is an object of reverence; each moment, even of the night, is sacred. Isis reassembles the corpse of her lover except for one crucial piece— the penis—which has been eaten by a crab or a fish. Undeterred, she has one carved, and, after Osiris is thus restored, and before he leaves once more to rule the underworld, entering entirely the world of the spirit, she conceives by him the child Horus.

The second integration, then, is fertile. The experience of coming apart and being all in pieces, and then the experience of being gathered mysteriously back into life: these are characteristic moments of the inner journey. The journey ends with a child, and so begins all over again.

The queen's act of gathering is the reverie of lovers and mothers. "Where is my child now?" murmurs the mother to herself. "Is she happy? Is she getting enough to eat?" Like Isis, whose blue cape reappears about the shoulders of Mary, the next Queen of Heaven, we muse and dream; the soul wanders and wonders, finding the pieces to make a human life, knitting up the bits of consciousness that have been scattered into the world.

During the process of mortification, the soul remembers and

recounts old legends, old wounds, old graces, and new possibilities and so gathers them and the breath of perfume that they carry. Othello wins Desdemona by telling his sufferings:

> She lov'd me for the dangers I had pass'd,
> And I lov'd her that she did pity them.
> This only is the witchcraft I have us'd.

Like the ancient mariner, we are under compulsion to tell again and again the heroism of our youth, the pains of childhood, stories of love and war. These are the shrines that Isis builds over the scattered pieces. In the same way, beloved names are sprayed on cement embankments under the freeways—in graffiti elaborate and enraged, colors bright with desire and misunderstanding. Falling in love has not made those painters more happy or more whole, but it has given them the incompleteness that begins a life. If something is broken, soul wants to sing about it and comfort it and mend it. The mother goes to the cemetery on the dead child's birthday and tells to the grass the story of the year on earth as if the child had not died but were away, travelling.

Purgatory, Again

The second descent into darkness bears a formal resemblance to the first—it too can be a shocking plunge in which our bearings are lost. First we are cast down, without regard for our bright achievements or intentions. Next, through surrender and compassion, we are delivered to traverse Purgatory. The initial anxiety, the difficulty, the feelings of loss and the anguish of walking the night road can be very similar. But there is a difference: we notice that this second darkness is more dynamic and less dense.

The first darkness is immobile, fixed, insoluble. In its grip we wait helplessly—putrefying, it seems, in our coffin; disintegrating into mere matter. We have to trust not in our effort, but in the unconscious forces of the world, in the chemistry of our cells, laboring to maintain us. Until the spirit shifts us, we cannot stir. The arrival of this spirit, this wind, seems to have nothing to do with us, yet it marks the dawning of awareness.

The images appropriate to the first descent, that painful birth, are those of Verdun and the Somme, where the troops of the 1914–18 war slogged through the mud and shell craters. Men shored up the floorboards in the trenches with frozen corpses and for the rest of their lives coughed out the mustard gas they had breathed in those years. They had no choice; they were in Hell.

In the second darkness we know again the sharpness of the inferno—yet this time we are not rudderless, and rudderlessness is, after all, the chief of hell's pains. Grief and sorrow are felt perhaps even more intensely, since we come to them now with more awareness, but when Hell has motion, its anguish will not endure. Fragments of light are scattered around like clues. To this second darkness belong those images in which each infernal realm has its own Buddha, appearing after the custom of the land—a little red creature with horns and a diabolic grin, but nevertheless a true Buddha, entering the realm to save the beings in it. And because this Hell does not last forever, it gathers to itself an atmosphere of modesty and repentance. Here repentance is not an abject surrender but a joyful elevation of our mood. Life's direction turns to the source, even during sorrow.

Carrying Stones

Repentance begs for burdens.
MICHEL DE MONTAIGNE

It is wisdom to find the tasks that are right for us at each moment of our journey. They may not be the tasks we hoped we should have, yet we must simply bear them. In Dante's *Purgatorio*, the souls carry great stones around the mountain paths and Dante, accompanying them, bends over in sympathy. But they hoist their loads joyfully, are glad of burdens and tasks because burdens and tasks will transform them. In Hell no one learns; even the most magnificent imp just repeats himself. At the bottom of Dante's *Inferno*, the greatest demon of all is frozen in ice. In Purgatory, though, there is movement, even if slow; and, because there is movement, the stars are visible, there is growth.

The purpose of carrying stones is to slow us down so that we may become present to our lives, so that we can enjoy carrying stones. The stones on our backs educate us through the dumb force of matter. The weight, the rough edges scoring our skin, the sweat running into our eyes, all these are the taste of life, the actual flavor of the Bodhisattva path. We carry the stones because we want to exist *in the world*.

One man's stone was AIDS. He had been treating it by weekly

consultations with a Chinese herbalist and by living a full life. The image he had was that of a liner going down—but slowly, on an even keel, while the music played. At the time, no treatment offered more than a brief, desperate prolongation of life, and he had seen friends die in misery, seen many funerals, many tears. He had always been angry about the disease, and had talked about suicide—sworn that he wouldn't die in restraints with his mind gone.

It became clear though, through the course of his illness, that his fear was not just about death—it was something he had always lived with. He had grown up with a sense of imminent doom: his father had worked at the Pentagon for the Strategic Air Command and a red phone had been placed in the bedroom for nuclear alerts. When there was an alert, his father would take off on the command bomber in case Washington, including his family, were destroyed. But even that was not the whole explanation:

> I have discovered I have the same feeling of terror and wrongdoing when I'm facing death and when the wallpaper comes off in my house. I've got hold of the live wire of my fear about life and I just have to keep holding on to it. In some ways it's harder than having AIDS, but I can do it. I just have to complete this process. I don't know what's the right way to go about healing my body, but I know I can do something about this sense that I've never been at home in the world. I don't know that I have enough time to heal my body, but I have enough time to heal my fear.

Carrying our stones makes everything alive around us—the hills, the trees, and the passersby in the street. Such labor keeps us out of Hell. When his dying time came, this man was no longer angry and had no thought of suicide. That night he drifted in and out of waking all night, his companion by his side. He waited till the stars began to fade at dawn and then he went. A little later, his friends came and gossiped and chanted for him in the hospital room as his body gradually grew cold. He had learned to be happy, carrying his stone: dying was putting it down.

The Spiral Stair

We seem alternately to transcend the human condition and to be utterly subject to it. The alternation *is* the human condition, as it is the natural alternation of moments of spirit and soul. That conversation constitutes our human life.

Our development sometimes seems so slow as to require geological metaphors—the breakup of Gondwana; the heaving and sliding of continents; the development of cyanobacteria to make oxygen; the migration of plants onto land, and then of the animals that followed them. It is as if we knew personally these majestic stages, in which great pauses are punctuated by sudden flurries of discovery and understanding. We carry in us so much that holds us back, and yet these are the very things that made us—the gill pouches in the mammalian embryo, the skeleton not quite adapted to bipedalism, the dark, uncertain memories from childhood.

We begin to see that there are rhythms and rhymes in the journey—the second darkness matches the first in a certain fashion and, in another fashion, is unlike it; later there will be other darknesses in which the rhyme will again form. It is this observation that leads to the image of the interior journey as a spiral stair. We come again over the same landings, where the same issues appear before us. Each time there is danger, a confrontation with the night. Yet each time there is also improved equanimity, a greater clarity, a briefer descent. Purgatory, like Hell and Heaven, is a moment we come to, time after time, on a particular turning of the stair. A Buddhist teacher put it like this:

> I began to realize that my happiness did not depend on being happy. I am always at a particular stage on the stair and my happiness consists of greeting my stage, even when it is painful, along with the knowledge that time turns all wheels and the next stage is always approaching.

We move like Isis over the delta of the inner life; the scattered pieces are collected and lost and collected again.

Regression for Growth

When we undertake a great new thing, an inner anxiety attends us. If we are true to our task we become incompetent—for all our learning is for the previous work, inapplicable now. It is as if we have to run the new way of seeing past the old problems. Whenever we have a series of very positive experiences, then we must look for the descent to come. This is not because there is some malign energy in the universe. It is more a rule of nature: darkness follows light and in turn is followed by light; a field must lie fallow; autumn must wither the stalks for the new corn to be planted.

Something in us must die before the new way can permeate our lives. That is what happens during the second descent. A composer and musician described his experiences like this:

> Whenever I am composing a new piece, it is the same. I have to go through the agony of not being able to do it. After I've suffered for a while, the piece opens up. I keep trying to cut out the stage of incompetence and misery, but it can't be done, and I'm not sure that I would want to do it. The blackness is the door of the creative process.

In inner development, this is an infallible law: we regress, breaking down the old rules, before we take the next step. In any creative process we have to go down into darkness before we can rise up. When we are humble, we don't claim or want to be other than we are: we enter our pain as the door to the next landing of the stair.

Humility

The Tao that can be named is not the eternal Tao.
    LAO TSE

Humility tries to be objective but still sympathetic to life. To be humble is to allow the world to strip us down—not to boast or to make claims; not to take success as an accoutrement of the ego or to take failure as a personal wound from the universe.

When we are humble, we accept that what sustains us is greater than we are and beyond our control, that the times of spirit and the times of soul, the times of gathering and the times of dispersion, are not always of our choosing. Humility assumes we are willing to work with adverse fate. It is close to the dark, accepting that from time to time we go down into night where the world may labor to change us, and that our goodness as human beings depends on accepting this descent. Humility is different from modesty, which is neutral and effortless and comes later in the journey. Humility, like meditation, is a discipline that makes an opening for joy.

A man has a chronic and intermittently debilitating illness into which he can relapse at the most inconvenient times—just when he is succeeding at a long-cherished plan, for example. Over the years he has grown cunning in his relationship with his body, as if taming a wild animal. This cunning is his respect and humility. When ill health—the feared visitor—returns, his first task is to welcome it. To simplify, to enter the illness, merely to have the illness without undue complaint, is itself a discipline and a kind of selfless prayer. Here is his description.

> Sometimes I have to spend hours just trying to let go of
> the idea that I shouldn't be sick, that what is happening
> shouldn't be happening.

This man has had to surrender to his sickness as a fate—not to quarrel, not even to want to quarrel, not to be on bad terms with the unwelcome guest. He has learned to consult it about his current level of activity, to be in connection with it as his instructor as well as his guard. It tells him about the quantity of his energy, the quality of his attention, the degree of freedom he may enjoy. Since this illness persists, the man cannot change his circumstances; yet sickness and confinement do not preclude happiness. To stay with, to undergo, to bless the present moment is to accept the new form of Purgatory. Softly and humbly he bends under the task.

The Joy of Human Hands

A man was sailing back in through the Golden Gate, on a mild winter evening at sundown, when his aorta split.

> At first it seemed to be a toothache, then the pain looped around my neck and seized me under my collarbones and I started to bend over. I felt a need to tell my friends, "I like life." It seemed to be a declaration of intent.

Under his instruction, his friends brought the yacht back, then the coast guard took him to a waiting ambulance. In the hospital, he was misdiagnosed at first, and tried to talk the physicians into letting him go home. But one of the doctors was uneasy; she ordered an echocardiogram for early the next morning, and it revealed that he was bleeding to death internally. He was rushed into the hospital at the University of California at San Francisco for surgery. As he explained in a voice still ghostly, touched by regions he had recently returned from, the most extraordinary thing was not the severity of being near death.

> I have always relied on myself. I have tried to help others, but have done things alone and it has always worked, more

or less. But here I could not rely on myself. I fell through the bottom, and hands reached out to catch me. Of all the events around my illness, that is the most shocking. That is what asks for the greatest change in how I see the world.

Through the mortification of illness and near death, soul emerged to make its claim on the man. Mortality gives us our tenderness for the common moments, the while of life. And we are always led back to love, and our beautiful helplessness, sustained as we are by what is larger than ourselves.

For our lives have a dimension greater even than Heaven—they are not just meditation, prayer, and moving through the clear, glassy air at dawn; they are also music, work, lingerie, fresh oranges, sitting with a friend through a long night of fever and drinking chocolate after. The spiritual work is not just to do the will of Heaven but to find out how to be human, to make a unique life. When we lean far in the direction of the spirit, mortification brings in the soul, which lends to spirit arms and feet. Soul is how we experience things in *this* body with *this* one life, the gift so precious and desperate.

The great things in life—death, love, birth—come at their own pace and do not consider our convenience; the best we can do is align with them. It is no use to complain, we must walk the road before us. In our humility we do align, we are like the mother who says, "I know the baby is coming," or the great theologian Paul Tillich, who woke up on his last morning and said, "Today is dying day."

The Fertility of Blindness

Humility leads us to trust, though we do not know where we are being led. When we trust, we accept a rich blindness. Tiresias, the Greek sage, experienced something ordinary mortals do not—the pleasure, if that is the correct word, of being in turn a man and a woman. But to go beyond the ordinary has its horrible costs and ironies: Hera questioned him about whether men or women had more pleasure in lovemaking, and when he offered his opinion that women receive more pleasure, the goddess grew angry and blinded him. As compensation, he was then given the gift of prophecy, of special sight. Tiresias in his blindness and the man whose aorta split open in his boat are like the young men in Australia when they are cut open during initiation, with clay or ash then packed in the wounds—they gain knowledge of the sacred ways, but bear the scars to their graves.

In the Zen tradition, it is said that there are many kinds of blindness. Mere ignorance is the first and most basic form. Blindness can also be the fruit of the work—an inability to see the illusions that govern most people, an incapacity that we might call profound blindness. When we rest in this kind of blindness, the world opens for us.

An acupuncturist who had trained in Japan once showed me a piece of calligraphy. It says "heart-mind mirror" in Chinese characters—a conventional subject. The idea is that the human heart-mind reflects the light of eternity, here and now. But this writing was wild, with an extraordinary depth of feeling, conveying both softness and power through the black ink. "The calligrapher is blind," said the acupuncturist. "He had been blind for fifty years when he did that piece."

Darkness is our foundation, the mysterious source of incapacity and blessings: we return to it again and again, whenever growth is needed. In blindness we surrender and rest in the empty, fathomless world, the nothing that holds us up. And when there is nowhere farther down to go, once again the countermovement begins and a task appears.

Paying the Dark

No good deed escapes punishment.
FOLK SAYING

Once the second descent is understood, we no longer try so hard to avoid the common course of human suffering, the routines of daily life, the blindness of the moment when we truly do not know what we must do. Wherever we are on our journey, it is good to acknowledge the dark. One way we do this is by accepting limits. In the practice of meditation we pay no attention to distractions, no matter how intriguing, following the advice Psyche was given when she went into the world of the dead. Such meditation turns us humbly toward the dark, and through it we pay for our journey, the way Psyche pays the ferryman and the terrible guard dog Cerberus. When we pay the dark, we save some place in our bright lives for confusion and melancholy; we keep open a door where the next moment can enter without having to force its way in.

In the ritual of a formal Zen meal, a portion of grain and a sip of tea are offered to the demons and spirits. It never hurts to appease the demonic and hungry parts of the soul, to have empathy for the neglected, the mad, the beggar on the street. In meditation, we offer our time—the fluid of our very life—to the demons.

There is also the custom of couvade, that anthropologist's favorite, in which the husband of a pregnant woman shares her labor, groaning and holding his belly while she delivers. This too is empathic. The man not only pays the dark and averts envy, he deepens his link to life, to the pains of birth itself and to the woman who bears the child. By sharing the woman's burden, he becomes receptive to her joy.

When something wonderful comes our way, it is good to do the dishes—not from a puritan rejection of joy but in order to make ourselves open to the increase of life; from an understanding, at least partly aesthetic, of the way balance occurs in the world and a desire to fit ourselves in with it. Sweeping the floor is also joy, the ordinary too is the unique. This is why when the student comes to the meditation teacher with a great experience of awakening, the teacher says, "Don't worry, it will pass."

To pay the dark is to carry the stone of our own suffering, asking for nothing. The courage with which we bear our darkness frees others from having to carry it for us. The task is not only to purify ourselves, to raise our affairs toward Heaven. Our sacrifice also draws the spirit down into our common lives, which is where it belongs. In this way the light penetrates, and the sweet colors stain us through. Then we find new guides: character and integrity, which mediate between the spirit and our human fate.

| # *Character and Integrity*

The Connections Between Character and Integrity

The marriage of Psyche and Cupid takes place in Heaven, above our daily world, and this union corresponds to our enlightenment or awakening. Like a wedding, this entry into the realm of delight is full of blossoms, sunlight, hope, and new understandings of our nature. And just as we hope that a wedding will bring a child into the world to carry the future, we hope that our new understanding will prove fertile. In this quest, we descend a second time and a third, and more, so that our awareness can be returned to the earth, where we were born and must live.

At ground level, spirit and soul set up house in the place we call character. The interior architecture of character gives us our unique shape, providing a vessel for the spiritual descent and ascent. Like a family house that gains rooms and skylights or loses a porch and stairs to the encroaching wisteria, character flows and alters during the course of a life. These changes are slow, but real. Character, as a container, gives us the ability to tolerate the mortifications necessary for the growth of awareness and for creative work. Character gives us the strength to hold both spirit and soul in the same moment, without entirely identifying with either.

Acting with integrity is the way we work with and refine character. The root of the word *integrity* means "whole or undivided," and so we think that in people with integrity their intention is not split from its embodiment—word and act do not differ, their spiritual impulses and soul impulses connect, and their life completes itself in the world. But we all have inner conflicts and so integrity must be something more complex than a lack of contradiction.

Integrity depends on our ability to set ourselves into the flow of life—to descend when it is time, to weep when it is time, to rise up again in joy when it is time—to do things, as in Ecclesiastes, according to the season. The ability to harmonize with fate depends on curiosity—on an interest in discovery, in finding out what kind of time we are in. We develop our integrity by testing a situation or a method—whether public or private. In such a test we do something and notice the consequences for ourselves and others; we are honest about those consequences and alter our future acts accordingly. In this way, integrity is realistic, grounded in the exploratory attitude we find also in research science, in the arts, and in meditation. This also means that there can be danger in integrity: that we can be unhappy and still be close to our integrity; we can make mistakes and cause harm to ourselves and others even though that is not our desire. Integrity thrusts us into the complications of being an individual in the great world.

Inwardness and Outwardness in Character

Most spiritual traditions acknowledge the importance of character and integrity. Its radical power is often lost, though, if we bring to that work too great an emphasis on heroism and certainty. As we have seen, humility is a lesson spirit must learn over and over—it is not natural to spirit's view. In *The Magic Flute*, even Mozart, a great lover of sensual beauty, saw the inner work as a battle with the Queen of the Night and the seductions of matter. Spiritual development has been variously described as rubbing stones together in a creek till they are smooth and round; as taking a bath to wash off delusions and impurities; even as going to the toilet, in the sense of purging ourselves—but such metaphors offer only the spirit's most narrow view. The implication is that life is somehow a false promise—the interruption of something more crucial—and, if only we can get rid of the body with its heartache, pleasures, and smells, and of the soul with its mortal yearning, then the eternal will shine through.

Spirit needs a link to daily life, something less drastic than its periods of mortification and descent. Character, receptive and enduring, provides the necessary constancy. It welcomes the multitudinous life and gives us a platform to stand on so that we won't be overwhelmed. Without such a foundation, we can preach a thousand sermons, pray for years, achieve ceremonial perfection, and learn the sacred books by heart, but alas, it all blows away in the wind.

Every culture builds some of the functions of character into its external forms, as a kind of exoskeleton for behavior. The rules that govern how we treat each other, the constraints all societies put on their members—these are part of an exterior container. The rigidity of this container relates to decisions a culture makes about tradition and innovation. Where tradition is foremost, the strength of the container is emphasized; where we love adaptation and the new, the container is more permeable and elastic.

Sometimes people can develop character by intense exposure to such external rules. Young men are often sent into the armed forces to teach them discipline, and, in some cultures, such as Thailand, monasteries have provided the same service. But large social movements to "improve the character of the nation," such as the 1920's attempt at Prohibition, are usually puritan regressions—projections, merely, of our own dark impulses onto others.

Fundamentalism leads to tyranny because it tries to avoid the uncertainties of inner development, referring every human action to a previously revealed creed—the dead bones of spiritual revelation. Part of the tyranny seems to involve an intemperate interest in improving and punishing others, and this passion, disguised as goodness, provides temporary relief from the confusion and remorse that belong with every life. Yet such thinking—so happy to attack the little sins—creates its own evils. For this reason it is important to wrest thinking about character away from fundamentalists. Character development, on the other hand, evolves slowly, from within, and brings with it relief and an experience-seasoned amusement about human flaws; it provides a gate for the spirit's boundlessness to appear in the soul's realm.

Setting the Container

Everything new needs to be held, needs a place into which it can be born. Copper requires great smelting pots to bring it out of the ore, a garden has a fence to keep out deer, the unborn child has the womb. The inner life too needs a vessel, a maternal structure. Character provides this matrix; it slows the harsh winds and also holds energy in, shaping the growing awareness.

To this vessel we bring our swirling selves. It cannot be completely sealed because we need to interact with life. We want it to be large enough to hold us, solid enough to bar the hostile winter sleet, penetrable enough for summer to enter with its bouncing light. The leaks have to be dealt with, but not entirely closed off. They cause pain and link us to the dark and that is their value— they allow the soul to enter.

We can understand what character is by noticing its absence. Where the container of character is not intact we find pain that seems somehow unnecessary and repetitive. The executive procrastinates beyond the point when any decision would have been better than none, the doctor takes painkillers when the problem is loneliness, the lawyer divorces her alcoholic husband and gets engaged to another man who drinks too much. Where character is structurally unsound, we do not seem to learn, we are terribly, glacially slow, and despair of changing our ways. Our most interesting passions seem calculated to destroy us, and it is as if there were a breach, a hole in the vessel of character, preventing it from holding whatever water we might pour in. We can eat and feel hungry immediately, be loved and stay lonely, be wealthy and feel the most desperate deprivation.

Perhaps you remember the story of a woman who fell abruptly into the experience of emptiness. She went in to her teacher, burst into tears, and told him, "Everything is gone; there's nothing left." "Oh, good!" said the teacher, but it wasn't good quite yet for her— her tears were not of joy and she was afraid. She was very new at meditation and had been chanting when her mind fell silent. The power of her innocent sincerity had led her beyond her readiness. Lacking a vessel, she did not yet have a way to hold her experience. She needed to wait, to have many ordinary, dull hours of meditation in which to experience the bounds of herself before she could break those bounds. Another woman described the necessity of waiting this way.

> There was a point in my life where I wanted to forget everything I had learned. I use the word *forget*, but what I really wanted to do was absorb it, to let it sink in, and not move on until I was ready.

When we have set the container by our long familiarity with our inner awareness, we can hold the life that pours into us. We will have weight, fertility, and endurance. When we are unhappy, we are not impressed by our pain; when we are happy, we are not disoriented by our good fortune. We just follow the road that opens before us, and when it is time to die, we just die.

Sometimes the greatest test of character appears when we face death. Here is a story from a meditation teacher that shows how the manner of a person's dying can be generous and steady, making a path for the generation to come.

> When my grandfather was dying I was seventeen. No one spoke much about it—perhaps not wanting to upset him. I saw him in his last day or so, and at first, I was shocked by the stench and the skin hanging in folds from his big bones. But he wasn't shocked. He was in considerable pain, wasting away, and the smell of his body dissolving was much stronger than the scent of the summer flowers in the hospital room, but he was steady with death. He talked about it matter-of-factly. The necessity of his departure was part of the understanding he had with life. "Yes," he said, "the pain is very strong. I'm ready to die now."

When it is time to die, we die, and when joy comes we need an equal equanimity. The woman who spoke of forgetting everything she knew tells about the rapprochement that came after the end of a beautiful but difficult love affair when the man's mother wrote her a warm letter.

> I just went immediately to do the dishes and remember saying, "Can my happiness withstand this dish? And this?" That day, when I was so happy, everything was usual except that I

was a little more careful because my feet kept lifting off the ground. That was my only task—to keep my feet on the ground.

Integrity

> *To realize the world of emptiness may not be so difficult, but to express the bare substance is hard.*
> JINGQING

To keep our feet on the ground is to find wholeness in our lives. We bring the spirit down into the world of soul to be embodied, to work, to be of benefit. At the same time we go the other way, too, bringing the world up toward spirit, ennobling the kitchen and the freeway.

Integrity is active, a practice concerned with motion, connection, and struggle. It does not just go by rules. In the great silence, integrity listens for the true course. This means that integrity is slow. It allows us to feel the anxiety of events developing, finding their shape; it does not rush through the time of growth, and enjoys the moment before the task is complete.

A practice is different from a skill, because it changes us as well as the world. The tasks of integrity are not personal accoutrements, like salmon fishing or speaking French with a Parisian accent. Many of us learn such skills without noticeable improvement in character. Yet an ordinary skill, such as fishing or speaking pure French, if learned as a practice, may itself become sacred work and help us to develop inwardly.

When integrity is a practice, we develop interesting tasks from our circumstances. A man with a successful career in advertising went back to school in midlife because he had never really learned to read or write well. He could get by, but a learning disability had prevented him from succeeding when he was a boy, and as an adult, his disability made presentations difficult. For him, the subterfuge that was necessary to hide his disability had itself become painful. His integrity was to notice and acknowledge this condition to himself and then to set out to change it. This meant sitting in classes with teenagers and refugees—it required the humility of admitting he belonged in the same situation as they. These steps—becoming conscious of a painful condition, being willing to call it our own, and then acting to change it—are essential movements of integrity. In this way the work of integrity requires the soul, with its affinity for darkness and humbling, and for acknowledging the pain in a situation.

On the other hand, as we age and gain power, it is dreadfully hard for us to keep our minds open, and to continue to learn. A spiritual teacher trained thoroughly and became the director of a famous temple. It is a pleasant spot, and he has the eye of a painter, so the grounds and buildings are deeply satisfying to walk through. He is also charming and wise and untouched by the sort of scandals and conflicts that nearly all spiritual centers have been affected by. But there is something excessively pure about the place, difficult to pin down. It isn't the Japanese swing to the roofs or the river view or the hardworking students. I think the odd factor is revealed in an event that happens again and again. The teacher attracts sincere, creative people who throw themselves into the spiritual work. Eventually he has a talk with one of the talented ones about becoming a teacher in turn and joining the tradition. The chosen student feels suitably honored and prepares for the work. But within a few months they have a fight about some lapse of the student's. The quarrel is so painful that the student leaves. The teacher is crestfallen for a while, and then begins once more with a new student. And the course repeats itself over the next few years. The curiosity that integrity brings, we might say the interest in error and impurity that integrity brings, is missing. In the pure shrine, nothing grows.

Here we can see how integrity connects to character. This is one of those unhappy patterns that we repeat because inside us is a kind of hole that does not mend, though we become famous for other skills and wise in other ways. Also we can see in this example that while integrity is an individual matter, it is not solely individual. Student and teacher are both implicated in a pattern greater than their personal intentions, a kind of shared disability, which requires movement from both parties.

Standing on Stones

Integrity helps us to find our place in the world. This is its durability, its irreducibility, its affinity with the stones that make up the earth's mantle. Integrity stands on the primal matter that we found through suffering. And because of its affinity with the stuff of the earth, it links us to our grandparents, the ones who are in the earth, and our grandchildren yet to come, whom the earth will produce like flowers.

At ancient campsites in the Sierras, there are mortars hollowed in the bedrock for preparing food. Integrity remembers the people who shaped the rock long ago, remembers its affinity with the unbudgeable stones. Such recalcitrance does not necessarily follow what everyone follows. To go against the current is a typical practice of integrity, which might lead us to prepare for war when everyone is hoping for peace, to resist war when everyone is beating patriotic drums. This obdurate quality appears in the words of a woman who left a relationship of which everyone in her circle approved.

> When I was living with S, I had everything I might wish for—a cultured, literate, sensitive millionaire. He smoothed many aspects of life for me. But I couldn't stay. I wanted someone who understood my passion for the spirit, and that was quite missing in him. It is not that he wouldn't have permitted my interests—he would have supported them. But it could never have worked on such terms. I am still poor and I struggle with my life. We are friends, S and I, and occasionally I get wistful letters. But I do not regret my choice.

In its stubbornness, integrity does not care about wealth, fame, comfortable circumstances, or the advice of friends. We must choose a fate of our own. The woman didn't dwell on riches or even kindness; not that wealth and kindness are to be slighted, but they were not enough for her at that time. Ultimately, such stubbornness is a kind of confidence.

Integrity can keep silent, choosing to ignore what it ought to ignore. In this way it protects us, insists that we live in this moment, which is all we have. One woman found out she was pregnant at the same time as she began to hemorrhage; she didn't lose the baby immediately, but it was clear that she would miscarry soon. There were medical reasons not to induce abortion, and so she was pregnant, but expecting the baby to die at any moment. She said, "I just can't go around not being pregnant. Each day I am pregnant until I am not."

There is nothing to be done about such a condition. The woman remains inside her situation, and this is the course of courage. And we can see from her example how integrity, so obdurate from one point of view, is also based on letting go. The stubbornness is humble. We stand on rock and what does the rock stand on? At the bottom of everything, the arms of emptiness support us and integrity depends on this emphatic insubstantiality, the strength of the invisible world. A woman continues to be pregnant until she is not. A meditator continues to practice though she does not know what the outcome will be. The man with bone cancer is alive and present until he is dead.

Things Said and Not Said

Whenever we care about our connection to the invisible, spiritual world, yet at the same time want to exist fully here, in the soul's imperfect realm, our integrity comes into play. We attempt to bring inner and outer worlds into correspondence by making a choice and bearing the consequences. If we are not all that we seem, we can put ourselves and others in a false position and we must bear the consequences, as we do in small ways every day, and in large ways during times of war and crisis, when survival itself may depend on dishonesty. Still, when we cannot be honest about our nature, like the man who concealed his illiteracy, we always seem to feel this condition as a wound—a matter of concern for our integrity. The move toward candor about our inmost lives is a move toward authenticity, which can be a relief, but is also a sacrifice. A learned businessman who is also homosexual described it this way.

> Coming out had consequences for me. There have been many jobs I didn't get. When I first came out, I was a member of the yacht club and everyone who sailed there turned his back on me. I wanted people to talk to and so I went down to Castro and 18th and there were plenty of people who would talk to me there. After a while, I didn't go to the yacht club anymore and my mother stopped being able to report my business successes to her bridge club. Most of the guys I went to college with are running large corporations now and here I am helping people dying of AIDS, doing everything from changing bedpans to raising funds for the new hospice. I'm insecure financially, and sometimes depressed about it. But I'm happy with my life; I wouldn't change it for being president of a company.

Here again, integrity is like a black stone, intransigent. It gives a ground to life through asserting a truth and suffering the consequences. This man has lost money and its security by his choice, and yet has gained in freedom, breathing the sharp, clear air of independence. For him, to be authentic is a great thing and worth the cost. Similarly, dissidents in some countries will give even their lives to preserve their integrity and the future hope of freedom.

We can see from this man's example that integrity, which stems from character, also alters character. We can lose integrity and weaken our character. If we go to the bar and drink whenever we are sad, then gradually we will stop being able to bear our sadness, and stop being able to bear our happiness, too. In a corporation, if we lie to our subordinates and never listen, and give ourselves raises while asking for sacrifice from below, after a while we will lie also at home and our children will fear us and will not want to sacrifice enough to learn what they must learn. The way we act when we are in difficulty is our answer to life's question, "Who are you and what do you love?" What we do then shapes our souls. In the same way, if we sacrifice and speak the truth when times are hard, others will see this and sacrifice in their turn.

The regular practice of meditation is helpful in this process. When it is boring, we learn to endure the lack of interest we have in ourselves; when it is exciting, we learn to be still and allow our excitement; when it is unendurably sad, we learn that we do not have to endure—we just need to breathe and weep and laugh in season while the grass pushes up out of the reddish-gray dirt and the wind carries our thoughts away. In this fashion, integrity shifts character; the holes in the container diminish and we become more effective in working with the stuff of the world.

The Knot in the Current of Time

In the world of time, complications always appear. Character likes slowness and desires us to wait. Waiting is not provisional time, servant to another moment yet to come—it is time in itself. It has its own elegance and disciplines. We wait so that we can catch up with ourselves, so that the rhythm can take shape before we start to dance; we wait because we can imagine far ahead of our ability to embody. A person arriving at a traditional Japanese monastery is turned away at first. It takes three days to get in. During that time, at best, we sit alone in a room, meditating; at worst, we stand in the snow. This is not a time to act, but to allow the world to act. During such days only inner events take place and so, invisibly, a transition occurs, as we move from outside the community to inside it. Afterwards, our actions and our appearance do not necessarily change, but everything has been shifted into the realm of the sacred.

When we are blocked, when circumstances are not ripe, we have to find some way of acknowledging that we are waiting, that we are pregnant and not merely asleep. Pausing like this is at the heart of meditation practice. When we attend closely to our lives, though it seems that nothing is happening, in the subterranean currents, reconciliation is setting off, invisible until the moment of its arrival. This waiting is not an effort at working a problem through, nor is it getting out of the way—it is being in the way just a little, just enough to allow the universe to work the problem through.

There is a moment when Jesus shows his mastery of such timing. In the story, a crowd has caught a woman sleeping with a man not her husband. They are angry and want to stone her to death. It is not clear why they ask Jesus to speak; perhaps they want his blessing on the murder, perhaps there is some unconscious doubt in them. Jesus does intervene but not straightaway—preaching to an angry mob is a ticklish business. At first he distracts: he draws on the ground with a stick. We are not told what he draws; it is the action itself that is important. This is an inventive gesture: it offers no answer, yet keeps the question in suspension. The crowd becomes unsure whether this is his response or not: a gap opens in their certainty. Time passes, and the moment becomes less fixed. Then, when Jesus speaks, the reproof in his words is indirect and points to the quest for knowledge. "Let him who is without sin cast the first stone." The men in the crowd are turned inwards and so walk away, each into his own destiny. Like other good solutions in desperate moments, this one came from nowhere, unpremeditated, given by grace.

In the inner life, readiness is one of the most important things. It is like a horse—the whole body has to turn toward the stream before she will drink. Our animal selves have to be aligned with the change. We have to be faithful to our lives—eat the cornflakes, write the memo, change the diapers, take the kids to the beach— and faithful also to that one small thing, which is the knot in the current of time, which brings awareness to our waiting. Our integrity is to observe these periods of waiting, the way in certain religious traditions the faithful observe fast days.

The forces of sleep and oblivion are so great that one conscious thing has to be in our lives every day: we need to touch the talisman that keeps us turned toward awareness. Meditation serves our integrity when it is with us daily. Then, when the horse lowers its head and begins to drink, everything will be changed. We can go through life ignoring the existence of that water, but once we have tasted it, we begin to orient our lives toward it.

Waiting in the dark allows us to rest until a solution comes out of the empty world. When we are impeded, we don't despair utterly, our waiting has a dynamic quality. Developing character can be odd work, since it often goes against our normal thoughts of advantage. A strange and successful example involves a friend who had a brilliant but capricious Zen teacher. Suddenly, after many years of training, he had had enough; furious with his teacher, he could no longer bear even to be in the same room with him. Some marriages are like this.

So the man went away and became a leader in his field, all the while working quietly on his spiritual life. Once a year he would go and, in the Asian fashion, bow to his old teacher. He was still angry and disappointed, and this action was the only thing he could find to do with the problem. Year after year he would bow and the teacher would be polite and the matter would rest there. This went on for seven years. Then the student came as before, but this time, inexplicably, his heart was light. It was as if a debt had been paid. It was like that for the teacher too. They laughed and embraced. Their relationship became simple.

This story has an elegant sparseness. Sometimes we can work

at a relationship too hard or in the wrong way. Sometimes we have to be patient, to trust the universe to sort out what is beyond our power. But the student did not just leave the matter to fate. He saw that this issue was not an incidental thing, not just a flaw in the road, but the road itself. It contained the problem of the flaws we always find in our mentors, the problem of the self-centered rage in the student that wants acknowledgment more than it wants life or truth, the problem of where to stand in relation to tradition, the problem of love between the generations, and the problem of how wisdom gets passed down. He saw that whatever his teacher's role, he had a task, too. In the eventuality, he was true to both sides of the situation. He didn't betray his anger, which had its own kind of integrity, and he didn't ignore the claim of the relationship, which was deep. He found an action, a spontaneous ritual that indicated to everyone involved—the universe, the teacher, and the student himself—that the issue was still in play, struggling to find its true form and to give off light.

This kind of ceremonial waiting both requires and develops strength of character. It is different from the pauses of earlier stages of the journey because it includes an awareness that holds even anger in a larger context of connection.

Doubt and Struggle

Traditional Zen practice is thought of as resting like an iron cauldron on three legs—one leg is doubt, one is effort, and the last is faith. Doubt is the first, and usually freely available in our culture. The contribution of the Zen tradition here is to point out that for the growth of awareness we must not ignore our doubts—they have great value, they allow us to penetrate, to see through the human situation.

To give attention to our current situation, including everything dubious and unresolved, is an act of integrity. In the later stages of the inner work, there is a temptation to ignore doubt, since so much seems clear. But fogginess is always with us, and to have integrity is to notice this. The story of Jacob wrestling with a being out of Heaven refers to such a moment of uncertainty. His life was in danger and everything depended on his presence of mind in the coming time. In the night an angel came and Jacob struggled with him. As the dawn came on, the man held on fast, and though he was injured in the hip, he would not let the angel leave until he had received a blessing. Integrity depends on our connection to the spiritual, but that relationship is not a simple or passive one. To earn spirit's blessing we have to be willing to struggle through on our own.

An example of staying with, struggling with, doubt and unease was given by an old Zen teacher, speaking about his own process:

> I ask myself, "What is bothering me?" And something
> pops up. Then I ask myself, "What is really bothering me?"
> Something else pops up. Then I ask, "What about under-
> neath that?" What's really, really bothering us is always
> mortality, the fragility of life.

Here, integrity is doubt pursued. Integrity asks what is real and keeps our noses to the grindstone. Its revelations come after inner conflict and hard work. Integrity embraces our natural qualms and the power of refusal—it leads us to reject everything comforting and offensive to reason, until the bottom of our inquiry is reached.

In this way questions become a treasure in themselves; they endure, and they are always fresh. Great questions get passed down as a sort of legacy, gifts for succeeding generations. In one of his Polynesian paintings, full of his languid amazement in the South Pacific, Gauguin raises up for our admiration and disturbance his eternal curiosity. He writes on the painting itself "Who are we? Where do we come from? Where are we going?" asking us, who witness and share his fate. We can respond to his questions only by holding them, pursuing them, living them through. Our questions keep company with our grief and happiness: we carry them along with us.

Bringing attention to our questions constructs the interior container of our character. But this work is not easy. We do not always pursue our question into its depth—we may accept a lesser question, yawn and distract ourselves, sink into oblivion.

In Zen, the student takes up a great question and perseveres with it, actively and incessantly, day and night. The question itself composes the subject of meditation, becomes the knot in the current of time. The student sometimes begins with a form of the question that has every appearance of absurdity—a koan such as "What is the sound made by a single hand?" That very absurdity contains the dark with the bright—the contradictions of being human. Or else the student may be given a naturally arising question, such as "Who is hearing that sound?"—the bird call, the truck passing, the voice of the world at this moment.

These great questions are full of night and cannot be answered in comfortable fashion. Preliminary, intellectual responses are rejected by the teacher until the student is drawn down to the bottom of the world. Persistent questioning takes away everything that merely seems solid until we are left with the underneath, the emptiness.

Using this method of deepening our attention, we sacrifice a certain complacency, but find a path composed of the questions that the universe has given us. This is deeply satisfying to our integrity, which does not want to gloss over the difficulties of leading a life of awareness. We enter our anxiety as if on a quest, learning to be attuned to our own uneasiness and even to doubt it, too. Doubt pursued to its ends, pursued beyond itself, strengthens character because it is something real. The method of questioning is full of beauty and terror. It does not pretend that the work of spirit and soul is pretty or easy, but it trusts the greatness of our human capacity to look life in the face. When we follow our doubt to the bottom, we are like Jacob; we hold fast to the angel until it bestows its blessing.

Effort and Perseverance

If the fool would persist in his folly he would become wise.
WILLIAM BLAKE

Effort is the next leg of the cauldron. To gather our fiercest effort may actually become more difficult as we progress along the journey, because the edge has been taken off our suffering. But the moment of effort, like the moment of doubt, does not belong to any one stage. Effort takes on the inner journey as a work that can be completed like other tasks. It develops the robust and achieving side of character by committing to the moment ever more fully. Effort wields meditation as a cutting sword, saying "No!" to everything that distracts.

Habits keep us unconscious and it takes effort to break them. Effort does this with its characteristic endurance and persistence. A habit is essentially an artificial limitation we have put upon ourselves because we cannot endure the newness of each moment. The shift from habit to moment-by-moment attention is described by an athlete who said:

> I used to overtrain because doing a lot made me feel like I was achieving something. It seems good to grind out the repetitions but actually it's just lazy. It's much harder to notice just what my body needs, how I'm breathing, but I do that now. And I never get injured anymore.

True effort is subtle. We can seem to be working hard but in truth be lazy because we are just sweating away without asking ourselves whether what we are doing is helpful or not. Such grinding is effort without integrity or doubt. True effort is harder and more interesting—it is present to each fragment of eternity passing through us.

Effort brings the fierceness of the outer journey to the inward. The energy of the soldier fighting in the jungle, of the dog chasing a ball, of the programmer up all night writing code, is brought to the development of character. Here we welcome the raw, fiery taste of life, stronger than whiskey—at once overwhelming and not to be refused.

As we progress, effort gradually becomes skilled, and cunning and settles in for the long haul—it brings to the perseverance cultivated earlier an intelligence and equilibrium. Good moments and bad come to flower, and die away. When we have found our strength through effort, our attention is sharply focussed and our character has weight; we no longer rise and fall with the stock market or the hopes of others. Our day-to-day effort then becomes a matter like writing a novel or learning the cello: the commitment seems large at first, but is at bottom a plain and common thing. It means merely to attend, to do the necessary work, to love the moments of which life is built.

Informing the Soul of Our Intention

The greatest part of effort is the mystery of intention. When we want to do something, we turn our hearts toward it and eventually a path opens. Much of the preparation for the inward work lies in developing the intention to do it, making it more important than going to a movie or being admired by our friends. It is not enough to long for freedom—we must have a platform in daily life, a basis for the change. Change itself is sudden, like harvest. It is preparing the ground that takes time.

The first moment of turning toward integrity is important because at that time, many of the elements of the journey are present in embryo. If we are hasty or tardy, if we neglect some part of ourselves, later we shall have to turn back for it. Acting with integrity serves notice to the universe that we do not neglect the beautiful and practical things we humans must do—the soul's tasks—and at the same time, that we trust in the mysterious unfolding of the spirit. The universe may bend toward us in invisible ways, but only if we are prepared to do without external help; only if we love the journey enough to persevere in the face of utter discouragement.

When Psyche was performing her tasks under her constraint, she just had to attend moment by moment to each one. When she looked ahead to the goal and opened the box from the underworld, she almost destroyed herself. The man who came to his Asian teacher and bowed each year had no guarantee that one day the tension would break and they would laugh together. He did not perform his actions merely for the sake of future results. What he did had its own virtue, the way a tree puts out leaves, saying, "Green, Green," praising life.

We walk and walk even though voices call us from the road. And we grow accustomed to the walking, which gathers to itself a dreamlike air. The Japanese word for a plain Zen monk is *unsui*, which means "clouds and water"—for eventually we flow, passing beyond intention, clinging to nothing while nothing clings to us. As doubt gives way to effort, so effort gives way to non-effort, drifting into what it has always longed for, what has always been the only way forward, in the brightest times and in the darkest— faith, the traditional third leg of the cauldron.

Faith and Listening

Doubt and effort, persisted in, strengthen the vessel that holds life. But faith releases us from the struggles of the realm of character and begins to join them with the freedom of the spirit again. It is part of character to know that there are things greater than anything we do, and that help can arrive though we had not looked for it. Jacob struggled with his angel all night. Nothing within his power could change the situation, so he had to endure. But then something changed in the world. Dawn came on. The desperate man was blessed and lived. The light opened his future.

Faith is the basis of inner work, since without it we might not persevere sufficiently in our doubt, or in our effort. Yet faith is also felt as a sort of reward, a fruit of the practice before we have any other visible evidence of the developing reality of the spirit and soul. With faith we relax; we don't have to push, the current carries us, even if we are in the dark.

Years ago, I worked for a brief period in the antique copper smelters in Queenstown, on the west coast of Tasmania. When the shift was inactive, the rule was that you had either to be invisible or look as if you were working. I would climb up into the girders, thick with sulphurous dust, and read Conrad's tales of the East Indies and the poems of John Donne, who loved women in the first part of his life and God in the second. I remember almost nothing of what I read, but that reading, its motion in the dark, is still vivid. I understood so little and yet, unconsciously perhaps, asked the poetry and the stories to change me so that I could enter their world. Reading in the girders was my act of faith: since I did not know where the journey was leading, I had to commit to it for its own sake, before even considering its goal. Such reading is a practice—like meditation on a question—in which if we persevere in incomprehension we are changed. Faith appreciates the absurdities of such a path toward growth.

To read was a struggle, not so much because I was dog-tired from swinging a sledgehammer to clean the furnace, but because I found that reading separated me from everyone around me. It separated me from the snow, the mud, the company bus stop, the pub, and the sulphur dioxide burning the hills down to their naked orange and pink. Later I would have to recover the world that was sinking away into emptiness while I hunched over my books, yet, in that time and place, merely to be reading gave me hope. I hardly understood the texts—sentences were comprehensible but the characters and the moves the authors made were opaque. I do recall reading a John Donne poem over and over and having the connections splash over me like sudden rain—noticing how his spiritual sonnets and his love poems worshipped the same force. I did not know at the time that reading was a discipline of the inner journey, but such knowledge wasn't necessary for it to transform me.

Faith is not belief. Faith is a charged waiting, a kind of sleep in which we dream. We are aware that our consciousness is lowered and that we understand little, but we accept this as an animal might accept the weather. We persevere without demanding very much except of ourselves. At first we just repeat our efforts—persistent, reverent, uncomprehending. With no natural gift, we listen to the music that the world sings all about us, we listen and listen and, gradually, patterns reveal themselves.

Faith has the force of grass finding its way up through the pavement. Faith sometimes looks like intention, but it is different: it hopes for no particular change, is content to continue until change is given and even if change is not given. When we have faith we follow the practice we have chosen, simply and with love; and how we feel about it, and whether our understanding has deepened yet—these considerations are none of our business.

Refining Integrity

If we do not listen to the voice of our integrity, we suffer. That suffering is a sacrifice to integrity, the way physical pain is a sacrifice to the health of the body. Both give us the information we need before we can change. To make the right decision is not essential to integrity—the point is to notice the consequences. In this way refining integrity is a step beyond paying the dark, where we merely accept that for the sake of knowledge we must give up our illusions and comfort. In the process of refining integrity, each decision teaches us. We notice and reflect. We learn to recognize that the next time we have a certain kind of queasiness it is not just something we ate; it is our true voice. This is humbling because what we notice first are the times when we act without integrity.

It takes courage to look at our deeds with objectivity, even when they occurred long ago. But without a sense of failure, integrity cannot develop. A woman told this story about herself as a twelve-year-old at summer camp.

> I had a friend with a physical disability and I betrayed her. She shat in her pants and at night the girls paraded by to look. I could do nothing. She wanted to sit next to me on the bus going home. Instead I sat next to a popular girl I didn't like at all. I was much more interested in my friend. I saw in my friend's eyes that she knew I was betraying her. Mind you, I suppose most girls of twelve wouldn't have stood up to that pressure, but still, I remember, I wince.

The important matter here is the unhappiness the woman feels at how she acted as a child. There were many reasons for that child's action—the barbaric pressure of the pack, and a sensible desire not to take on the sorrows of the world just yet—but it was a betrayal nonetheless. It doesn't seem possible to develop integrity and to refine it without the dreadful example of our own failures.

Turning Failure About

> *By the earth we fall down, by the earth we stand up.*
> SHUNRYU SUZUKI

Integrity is independent of success in the world because while it mediates with matter, it does not identify with it. If we act with integrity we develop our character and put ourselves into the right relationship with eternity. This course prevents us from sabotaging ourselves and so may bring success in the world. But we can be born into times and places that make success very difficult. This is entirely acceptable to the person of integrity. One can take either the inner or outer road to happiness, and if the outer is blocked, it may well help us attend more closely to the inner.

In the Chinese wisdom book the *I Ching*, the situation of general difficulty is called *Chien*, or Obstruction: it gives the image of being hemmed between a watery abyss before and a mountain behind. It doesn't matter what the obstruction is—a death, a divorce, a wrecked business deal. When we are blocked in the outer world, the *I Ching* suggests it is best to wait and to use the dark time for character work.

> Water on the mountain: The image of OBSTRUCTION.
> Thus the superior man turns his attention to himself
> And molds his character.

A young couple were central figures in a small community. They had fine children and were much admired. Then the marriage came apart in a whirlwind, a true mortification. The woman was vilified by her friends. She felt herself unable to judge what was what, but felt the pain of isolation and was ready to believe that she was to blame. But she was also a veteran of meditation, a qualified teacher, and decided to use her anguish as an opportunity to deepen her spirituality. In the midst of her crisis, she went to study with an older teacher.

> Before I came to him, I'd had many spiritual experiences. But I knew I had reached some sort of limit. He questioned me

closely and I answered him with confidence. But he rejected my answer! He said my understanding wasn't deep enough and kicked me out of his interview room. And when he did this, I had a strange reaction: I was excited, I was happy because here was my chance to go deeper. I will always be grateful for that "No!" which respected the crisis I was in, grateful that he took me so seriously.

Whenever we are defeated, two reactions hover near us—grief, and excitement for the opening of doors.

The ability to turn about, to change course, especially if we have a lot invested in our current direction, is a basic element of developed integrity. This ability is much more important than not making mistakes. The same teacher this woman sought out, who is now one of the grand old men of Zen, tells a similar story from his own early days of teaching. After many years he had completed his formal studies in Zen. He returned from a visit to Japan, and he was met with much excitement by his students, who gave him a book, newly published, of Zen essays by an old Japanese master. During his first retreat as an independent teacher, he read this book. Many years later he said,

> I could tell immediately that it was a good book, but I didn't understand it. My incomprehension horrified me. It meant my training was not complete and yet my students were bowing to me and calling me "Roshi." I felt ashamed. Well, as soon as that retreat was over, I picked up and fled to another teacher, a man younger than myself, and became a student again. He was very generous to me in public, and gave me a

place of honor in his temple, yet privately pressed me very hard. I didn't leave for home again until my understanding had cleared up.

Here we see the same ability to turn failure about that he later evoked in his gifted student. His understanding did not meet his own requirements, but instead of despairing, he acknowledged his situation and sought a remedy. Integrity at such a moment involves acknowledging a problem (having great doubt), not being utterly disabled by shame (having great faith), and persevering (having great effort). There is a traditional Christian story about this turning about:

> A monk looking for some guidance and encouragement goes to Abba Sisoius and asks:
> "What am I to do since I have fallen?"
> The Abba replies: "Get up."
> "I did get up, but I fell again."
> "Get up again."
> "I did, but I must admit that I fell once again. So what should I do?"
> "Do not fall down without getting back up."
>
> VERBA SENIORUM

Turning about is related to the ability to see the path as something that goes on and on, with infinite vistas. Our faults are always large and visible to all; compassion and perseverance are always necessary. Somewhere in the universe, the Chinese say, the Buddha is still deepening his enlightenment.

The Cliff

Jumping off the cliff with open hands
Wumen Huaikai

Often we just don't have enough information and yet must make a decision anyway. The matter may be one of life and death, and still all we can do is make the best of it—decide, according to our heart, our courage, and our generosity. We can then watch to see how well things turn out, but we shall never know how it would have been if we had chosen another path—married another person, picked a different career, fled a war we fought, fought a war we fled. We are mortal, life is limited: facing these truths requires the development of our character in the first place. Choosing without sufficient information, we enter life completely, and that is our action of integrity. A man spoke of his experience during the Vietnam War, many years ago.

> Now it seems clear that the war was wrong, but at the time we weren't so sure. It seemed to be a pointless military adventure, but I felt obliged to volunteer, because I knew men who had gone and been badly wounded, and I thought I should go out of loyalty to them. Every time I walked past the draft building I winced. Also, I had a South Vietnamese friend who was a student with me, son of a colonel.
>
> In the end, even though I could have got a conscientious objection, I became one of the early draft resisters. I left school and the glittering career intended for me from childhood. Now I think that I was torn by conflicting vanities—

the pride of going to war, the pride of standing against the giant machine of war. At the time, I wasn't sure, but I had to decide anyway.

This man had to decide, without good information, a course that would change everything about his life. The process of developing integrity is still going on—thirty years later he is still holding some of the questions open. To choose is to bear the shame, guilt, and incompleteness that come from action; to choose is to make errors and to live.

Compassion as Sacred Work

The best way to combat evil is not directly but to make active progress for the good.

I Ching

Good character doesn't happen by accident. We develop our character through the undertaking of tasks, knowing that we do so both for ourselves and for the world. Our tasks enlarge the wide day. With good character we are tough inside, but pliant outside, able to be rigorous and helpful.

The woman who came to the old teacher and deepened her spiritual path eventually returned to her community. Her exhusband was living with another woman, previously a close family friend, almost next door. This became a new task for integrity. The woman had carefully examined her own part in the breakup but she had not expected to be abject and jealous.

She realized that she had to stop looking to see if his car was there, arguing with him in her head, wishing she could make him understand. She did not want to plead with him, she did not want him to have anything to do with how she felt. So she took up the meditation of compassion. It was hard at first; she felt a kind of chaos within. But she fought it by saying to herself the ancient impartial words "May I be peaceful, may I be happy. May my child be peaceful, may she be happy." Then, as her mind settled a little she would extend the wishes, the feelings of warmth, to her ex-husband, to the new woman, and so, gradually out beyond—to the trees and the ocean. At first, entering compassion was hard work, but returning over and over to that arduous meditation made her strong. Gradually, equanimity came.

Over the next fifteen years or so she became a leader in her world. She never felt that she had understood what had happened, but the old disaster of her marriage had transformed itself into a benign force. The practice of compassion detaches us from our heavy emotions so that when they arise they do not capture us. We are free of wanting things to be other than they are.

By the influence of compassion, the soul is included in the work of integrity. Without it, integrity might be seen merely as a set of rules or as a series of stern tasks, as in this old Chinese story:

> A scholar told Confucius about a man who reported his father for stealing a sheep, praising this action as an example of integrity. "Where is the integrity in that?" Confucius replied. "The son covers up for the father and the father covers up for the son—that is integrity."

The catalyst, in such a case—the quality that integrity implies and needs—is human connection. Integrity must bear the secret kindness of life as well as carry our anguish, must be faithful to our joy as well as to the pains we bear. Carrying such kindness makes us vulnerable—to the softness of life, its seductive pull into form and mortality, and the doomed quest to savor and delay time. It makes our character permeable, makes character into the house that keeps out the rain and lets in the sun, the house in which the windows are open and children laugh in the corridors.

Chapter 10

Gifts from the Source

Doing Nothing

The great way is not difficult,
it just avoids picking and choosing.

JIANZHI SENGCAN

There was a soldier who practiced Zen. When he meditated, the stillness was so profound that the house itself grew silent, the mice and even the crickets were quiet. When his wife mentioned this to him, he said, "Well, this won't do, I'll have to try harder." So he gathered his attention, and as his meditation deepened, the mice began to play happily around him, even jumping on his clothes as he sat, serene and joyful.

We often forget the value of allowing the night and the day to flow in and out of the house while, on the hillside, the grass grows by itself. In general we are not lazy enough, and struggle too hard. Anyone can achieve things but really to do nothing requires resolve. To become one with sitting is to become one with walking, with working, with jumping about, with being sad, with falling in love. The world goes its way, spring, summer, autumn, winter, and we are at home. What our integrity leads us to do then is what the old Chinese teachers called "the things of Buddha"—eating, drinking, laughing, feeding the children, weeping, burying the dead.

The man whose aorta split open at sea said that when he was recovering after his surgery, he noticed something:

> The habit body, the opinions and thoughts that I normally carry around, was quiet. Usually they make a kind of veil, or a buffer over things. But they were silent. And that was very nice.

When we let drop the veils of our usual preconceptions, we are closer to our lives, sustained without knowing why. When we cannot see how healing or the next step in our lives will appear, and no longer know what we can expect, the step we must take just emerges, out of nothingness, like the grass. What rises to meet our need comes from a domain deeper than the realm of custom, more ancient, beneath our feet and our awareness, thousand armed, beyond our control. To live without veils, in modesty and unknowing, is to trust to the abyss, as a swimmer trusts to the ocean, and gently moves both hands and feet; it is to flow through the days like boys on a raft down the Mississippi. The old Chinese teachers called such activity "doing nothing," or "not-doing." This doing nothing is an inner event that can take place in strenuous action or utter stillness. To do nothing is always harder than we imagine.

Not-doing, in which we lounge around and loaf at our ease, is a kind of falling out of our lives, the way when his aorta split the man fell through and beyond his habits. Visible and invisible hands reach out and we find that we have always been supported by much that is unknown and beyond our plans. Just as Alice, in the surprising, uncontrollable moment of dropping down the rabbit hole, found a marmalade jar on a shelf, we meet common things in a field of wonder. The orderly progress of breakfast, lunch, and dinner catches us and there is the beauty of work, tea, jam on toast, the body's cabinet of pains, the quick feet of rain scratching toward us over dry leaves.

Unlike ordinary laziness, in which we merely avoid something we think we ought to be doing, the laziness of not-doing has a refined and charged quality. By comparison, ordinary laziness is hard work and requires distraction. When we truly do nothing, a fertile, widening silence appears. Close to the mystery, we drift along. There is no resistance to delusion, yet delusion can find no ground to cling to. In the midst of action we rely on the stillness that is everywhere present. If the world is imagining itself without our assistance, why then, we let it do so. When we truly do nothing, we allow that falling can be good, that arms might catch us when we do fall, that the world may sustain and surprise us at the same time. We respond naturally, witnessing the web of life of which we are a part, just as water runs downhill and the white clouds run before the breeze.

After a certain point, knowing and effort don't bring us into closer harmony with eternity; our love for fragile creatures provides a route. Francis of Assisi spoke with the birds. The Japanese poet Issa was concerned for the little forms of life:

> Don't worry, spiders,
> I keep house
> casually.

Not-doing, having no urgent plans, we dawdle in the intimate while, like a child jumping puddles on the way home from school. The world comes to us then, and we belong in it, in the morning light at the equinox, with the hawks swinging on the updrafts over the headlands and, in the afternoon, with the fog rising out of the ocean to fling itself, kraken-like, onto the towers of the Golden Gate Bridge. At last we are at home in this fleeting life.

The Bodhisattva's Thousand Arms

> *Though you find clear waters ranging*
> *to the vast blue skies of autumn,*
> *how can that compare*
> *with the hazy moon on a spring night?*
> *Some people want it pure white,*
> *but sweep as you will,*
> *you cannot empty the mind.*
>
> KEIZAN JOKIN

To live in the flow of doing nothing is to connect spirit and soul without surrendering too much to the demands of either. The

Buddhist concept of the Bodhisattva offers an image of spirit and soul *coming together*, of clarity and love conjoined in an integrity of being. The Bodhisattva does not transcend the world, but remains within its turmoil to work for the enlightenment of all.

Early in the journey, we often hold an ideal of the inner life that contains a great deal of perfection, certainty, and purity. Now, with the integration of soul, we have grown most interested in the illumination of compassion and in a modest participation in the fate of other living creatures. The later ideal includes as well a joy in our helplessness, in the nakedness that gives so sharp a quality to being human.

One popular Asian image of the Bodhisattva is of a fat, jolly old man with a sack—the natural human as a spiritual being. In appearance, he is curiously near to Falstaff, our Western assemblage of appetites, whose sack is his belly and who would eat and drink up the world if he could. The Asian figure also has a connection to the animal life but, unlike Falstaff, is serene and unattached to its delights. The sack is a cornucopia and all the world is in it. In particular, there are sweets for the children who surround the old man, like bees about a trellised rose. The presence of the children tells us that our effort is not devoted to scorning the world but to tending it. Jesus, too, asked the children to come to him.

The Bodhisattva's intimacy with life means that his speech is composed of many voices—there are many people in the sack. We have to be ample enough to include a wide possibility of being and still hold to a central core. During the Second World War, before he was a venerable Zen teacher, Robert Aitken was in a prison camp in Japan. There he met the translator R. H. Blyth and asked him, "How do you save all beings?" Blyth replied, "You save all beings by including them."

The most miserable refugee, the prisoner in chains—no human being is beyond the interest of the Bodhisattva, or beyond the possibility of developing into a Bodhisattva. Even non-human beings—snakes, wallabies, and Tasmanian devils—can be Bodhisattvas, touching us to the core and opening our hearts. There are always Bodhisattvas among us, helping, visibly and invisibly. They teach us, console us, serve the sick, the poor, and the lost.

Now, the essence of the Bodhisattva's story is this: she has postponed her own ultimate enlightenment. Liberation would mean leaving this world with its anguish, never again to be bound upon the wheel of birth and death, and, in her compassion, she has taken a vow to remain in our company, guiding us to safety, until the last of us is free. She hears our cries and weeps with us, and while any creatures are left to suffer she will not go on. She wants to enlighten the least of beings, even the hills and the grass. With us, she enters the place of the small, the personal—the realm of soul.

The Bodhisattva's legend includes the timelessness of the inner work, the sense that when we meditate, we connect with aeons of past human effort, the slow struggle out of darkness. There is the sense that the journey has taken thousands of lifetimes and that we have developed with nearly infinite slowness, up from the level of single-celled creatures afloat in the primeval soup, up from the mollusc level, up from the first swimming vertebrates. We stand upon so many ancestors, we have had so many mentors and our mentors have had mentors, and so into the distant past, many lives.

As we develop and rise, we see the value of all these conditions of being. We do not use our consciousness in an escapist way to separate ourselves from those who work and suffer, to think of ourselves as superior to the animals and the rivers. If we entered completely the ideal realm, the upward escalator of awareness would take us beyond our world and our tenderness for its struggling beings. But the Bodhisattva refuses the temptation to identify with pure spirit, to be free of the pains of life, of choice, of earning our food by our sweat, of giving birth through travail, of the tremor of unfulfilled desire, and of the disillusionments of satisfaction. The Bodhisattva recognizes the dark side of spirit—if we are buoyed up into eternity, we lose concern with our own humanity and cannot help others.

So, for reasons of the soul, the Bodhisattva chooses uncertainty and imperfection, bending toward us and our suffering. A paradoxical and fully human creature, she is only whole if she is also incomplete. We might assume that the more purely we entered spirit, the more we would be able to help others. But this figure shows us that the opposite is true—we are linked to life through what is partial. This is an improvement over our usual ideas of holiness, in which the saint is seen as impervious and untouched by the world or else as luxuriating in a kind of orgy of renunciation, like Saint Sebastian chock full of arrows. One Zen myth tells of a disciple who, to prove his sincerity, cut off his arm, and stood waiting in the snow. This heroic gesture (though it too creates an incompleteness) is typical of the stripping down of the spirit—the priests who flog themselves, the villagers who have themselves nailed to a cross every Easter. But the Bodhisattva, who does not split soul from spirit, is not ascetic or harsh. Her thousand arms bring the sun up in the morning and carry us to our rest at night.

Bodhisattvas can be of service because they have a gap, an opening through which we meet them. Through their weakness, they are bound to the world we move in every day, with its dreams and broken hopes, its blood, sorrow, and generosity. They show us that our transformations, too, arise out of the place where things are not whole or satisfactory, the place where we suffer.

We can notice the truth of the Bodhisattva's way in our daily lives. When we suffer, we can grow sweet. A business executive who was in turmoil in her personal life noticed a paradox—that people seemed to connect more easily to her now, and to ask more readily for her to help them.

> At a time when I am in greater internal confusion than ever before, people are turning to me for help. I used to be rather dry, but I can't manage that anymore. I feel for the people who work for me and they can tell. On the other hand I feel a loneliness which I didn't notice before. I have more empathy, and I am also more aware of my own pain, and I know that I have to come to terms with it myself.

Every step into awareness means letting go of an old way of being, and the unavoidable grief of that change is loneliness. With its special talent for mourning and delight, the soul enters us through cuts in the healthy flesh. When we are in pain, it is amazing how much tenderness we are capable of, and how much joy we can take in the happiness of others. Even our anguish is one of the engines that preserves the world, and makes possible our human joy. Only angels and monsters are always strong and transparent of conscience.

An old Chinese saying asks:

Why is it that perfectly accomplished Bodhisattvas are attached to the red thread?

The red thread is the road of passion—of sorrow, love, sex, adoration, grief, intimacy, uncertainty. If we love deeply, we make an invisible bargain with the one we love—a bargain that goes like this: "Either I will be at your deathbed or you will be at mine." Love's companion is parting. We know that love ends in loss but also that loss is itself full of richness—the irreducible touch of skin, the voice of the owl, invisible in the high eucalyptus tree, past midnight, when the moon has set and everything else is still.

There are paintings of Hell realms in which the Bodhisattva appears in the fire, with horns and a red face. From one point of view she has entered Hell to save even the demons. From another point of view, even Hell is beautiful to the one whose heart is at rest. If we are incomplete, there is room to learn.

Through our wounds the light pours in, and the task of consciousness is to mirror it back so that gradually, over millennia, human awareness increases. Each of us does a small part of this grand work—mapping the course of the eternal road in our time.

At this stage of the journey, integrity is a willingness to rest in the incomplete, the partial, the emerging, the unformed.

Loving Whatever Is Incomplete

Soul and spirit, like other opposites, tend to express their own separate natures. At first in our journey, for the sake of clarity, we have to recognize and even encourage this division. At that time, we are like Psyche sorting the seeds. As we go on, though, there is something suspect about such opposition. For, as well as a fissile pressure, soul and spirit have a natural companionship, a predilection for conversation, a shared delight in the unfolding moment.

After travelling their long-separate paths, soul and spirit draw toward each other again because each has what the other lacks. They seem now to *want* to mingle, and when they do, the experience is deeply ecstatic. Illuminating each other, they are beautiful but difficult lovers. Secretly, spirit wants embodiment, wants to sink down and be mortal, to bleed, to struggle with high blood pressure and menstrual cramps and cold toes. Without these pains, spirit is ghostlike, vague, adrift without links to the earth. And the soul, which knows more than it needs to about the fragility of the body, secretly loves weightlessness, the voice of the soprano, rising like the lark vertically above the tussocks at dawn. We need both realms. We are at once vast and tiny, intensely personal and at peace.

Honoring what is incomplete, we must love our lives in their details: the puzzling marriage and the child who likes to read, the smell of melting asphalt in summer, the wistful pleasure in the autumn mist that gives its nobility to the procession of cars. Soul and spirit hold their conversation within these moments, and their conjunction is the embodiment of enlightenment. By holding soul and spirit together, we rescue love for the spiritual world and allow earth to be enlivened by Heaven. The ingredient of soul in the compound permits the outpouring of compassion. Heaven, in turn, is given weight and zest and the terrifying beauty of mortality. When the two interpenetrate, then there is a harmonious state of affairs; the child plays, the summer afternoon goes on and on.

In the *I Ching*, it is not a good condition when Heaven is above earth. Each realm recedes from the other into its own pure nature, and less and less becomes possible. The spirit flies up and the soul plunges. Then we have to wait, and worry out the time until it changes. This is the hexagram of Standstill, in which there is no intermingling. On the other hand, when earth is above Heaven, we find the situation of Peace. The heavy earth sinks and Heaven rises through it. They interpenetrate and inform each other. Nothing is perfect or pure, but all things are right.

A woman had her bathroom remodelled by a Japanese-trained carpenter. It was slow, precise work, requiring bent wood and odd angles, and each detail was perfect, it seemed. But when he had finished, he took her into the room and asked her to bend down and look into a dark corner. He had left a flaw in the skirting board, a slight and deliberate error. This is an ancient idea. It stops the gods from being envious and acknowledges that in our human realm, imperfection allows life to flow in, making a path for happiness and human uses. In such a gap, uncertainty becomes a surprise, a wonder. We are ready to fall into it, as if into happiness itself.

The Mystery at the World's Core

Every great question generates its own thick umbra, which requires of us our waiting, the passage of precious months and years. The Bodhisattva's integrity appears when we hold to uncertainty, enduring the inner struggle. Then we are pregnant with waiting, groaning with waiting, until time comes to aid us and the new way is born.

In a letter to his brothers, the poet John Keats wrote about living inside the mystery:

> It struck me what quality went to form a Man of Achievement, especially in Literature, and which Shakespeare possessed so enormously—I mean *Negative Capability*, that is when a man is capable of being in uncertainties, mysteries, doubts, without any irritable reaching after fact and reason.

Along with uncertainty, Keats is embracing the essential insolubility of our dilemmas. The Bodhisattva's imperfection appears as a not-knowing, an openness in our innermost hearts. This condition will not clear up eventually; it is a truth of our nature.

At a certain point, even our wisdom can be an obstacle to growth. In the inner work, as in diplomacy, it is sometimes better not to make things clear. When we have the mind of beginning, things are unformed and still vigorous. The inner work increases a kind of positive blindness. We become blind to the world, we meditate instead of going to the beach. At the same time, our blindness offers freedom, just as it brought to Tiresias, the blind seer, special knowledge of fate. We are like the child who sees a vision of the Virgin while reciting the prayer "Hail Mary full of grapes"—our not-knowing seems richer than our certainty.

One of the foundation stories of Zen Buddhism shows how it is to rest in indeterminacy. Bodhidharma is the semi-legendary person who brought the meditation tradition from India to China long ago. Shortly after arriving in China, he was summoned before the emperor Wu of Liang:

> The emperor, who had endowed many monasteries, asked, "What merit have I earned?"
>
> "No merit," said Bodhidharma.
>
> The emperor then asked, "What is the first principle of the holy teaching?"
>
> Bodhidharma replied, "Vast emptiness, nothing holy."
>
> "Then who is this before me?" asked the increasingly puzzled ruler.
>
> "I do not know," said Bodhidharma.

We can say nothing about the mystery directly. Yet every day we move into it and through it and are sustained by its graces. When we are disciples to its ways, the nothingness beneath our feet befriends us. Darkness comforts, not-knowing is a plenty. In our blindness we trust, we depend on what lies beyond the limits of awareness. Because we are not blocked by our seeing, we are like convalescents, we feel the thousand arms of Kuan Yin bearing us up. Bodhidharma's integrity is to claim nothing, so that he can embrace whatever comes.

Falling Asleep

Falling asleep is a traditional image for coming into accord with our not-knowing. It is like doing nothing, but goes even deeper into the dark core, allowing the imagination of the world to work through us, the way in actual sleep dreams appear. Such sleep is without the element of struggle and sacrifice characteristic of the early descents; it includes darkness and blindness as its fertile ground. To fall asleep in this way is to fall into eternity, into the Tao, into the realm of magic and surprise. It is lucky, allowing time to pass and the universe to come to our aid. Old paintings show the sage Manjusri, asleep on the flank of his companion the lion, also snoozing. In the ballads of the Scots border, young men and women fell asleep on a hillside and were taken into faery land for seven years.

Here is a writer's experience of that surrender, of being overcome by her own inner life.

I sat down to work on my novel and had such resistance, I couldn't prop open my eyes. I conked out for twenty minutes. When I woke I had to force myself to sit at the desk. But then a whole scene just came.

There is a close relationship between darkness and the creative. This does not mean that artists must be drunks or even unhappy—that is a sentimental idea. It is just that the way up leads through the way down.

When we step into a new moment or a new work, we do not have the abilities we need because we do not know what we need. We feel inferior, heavy, hopeless. We may think that we have no ability at all and indeed, that we never did have a genuine talent. Through these emotions we enter once again the descent. Eventually we discover anew that the thing to do in the night is to sleep—to give ourselves over to compassion, to harmonize with the dimness about us—and then to stumble back into awakening by taking up our given task, and so we do: we work. The musician plays, the nurse sees patients, the broker makes trades, the pilgrim meditates. We persevere—exhausted, despairing, slow, wading through mud. The malign angel of the mood presses like the grave on our chests. Accepting such heaviness, we find that we are content—to be helpless, foolish, without hope. In such contentedness we rest, as if in a hammock, as if in our mother's arms. Through this resting, we are reborn: doors open, branches of light come streaming through the dark. Then we are competent again. The air fizzes, the mountains are alive, we have achieved the new moment.

It is said that the last calligraphy of the great Zen teacher Yammamoto Gempo was the character *dream*. How distant is the past and the future, how insubstantial all that we have done. Even our crimes grow vague in retrospect. Dream provides a necessary cloudiness to the data of the senses. We dream the world and ourselves into being, and the wisps and banners of eternity still cling to us, as an irreducible freshness. Chuang tse dreams he is a butterfly and wakes to question his life. "Am I a man," he asks, "who dreamed he was a butterfly, or am I a butterfly, dreaming that he is a man?"

To bless the imperfect, to enter the not-knowing, is to make a voluntary return to darkness, the source. Descent into mystery is a late form of the plunge into night. Mystery is what we don't know, what doesn't fit, what we have not made into shape and order; it tells us that surprise is at the core of life, terrifying but also delicious.

The Awkwardness of the Real

If we look at an elk it is not at all like the idea of an elk. It is not cute, lissome, or elegant. It has ticks on its neck, its coat is patchy in summer, and the way it stretches its leg and looks back over its shoulder is beyond admiration. The difference between the animal and the idea of the animal is awkwardness.

To relish the imperfection of actual being is a form of integrity that is anchored in the senses. Like other happinesses, it is its own discipline. It provides a vessel for the imagination that doesn't appear if we are just making things up without reference to the genuine strangeness of life. When we embrace awkwardness we enter our own lives. Cinderella is better prepared for the world than her stepsisters because she sweeps and sews—particular, inconvenient, unromantic activities that develop her character. From that foundation, her imagination and her naive and discontented dreams can flow out of the little cottage and up the steps of the palace. Awkwardness is a discipline that has set her free.

In its origin, *awkwardness* means "a backward motion," and whenever the spirit is rushing ahead and projecting out toward an ideal, a backward motion steadies us, drawing the soul in. The experience of awkwardness is twofold, beginning with a sense of shock. "This not what I expected," we think. Then, as we continue to gaze, we see, "But it is true, it belongs, it is more real, it amplifies me." We find in ourselves a tenderness for what is revealed even though we did not seek it. In just this way the common griefs of life bear the enlarging sting of awkwardness to us, breaking the spell of routine unconsciousness. As character and steadiness deepen, what would have been a trauma at the time of the second descent becomes something to observe, a wave of the universe.

The old Chinese teachers used to try to reproduce the surprise of the real, using shouts or blows. One of the greatest of these guides, Linji, three times asked his teacher the same question about fundamental reality, and three times his teacher hit him. Uncertain what to make of these events, he told his story to another teacher, saying, "I don't know whether I was at fault or not." The second teacher said, "He exerted all his grandmotherly kindness and you come asking whether you are at fault or not?" and with these words Linji had a great awakening. It is easy to think of the teacher's blows as obscure and in the past, as awkward in fact, but this story came to the aid of a woman when she was buffeted by the transience of life.

As my father was dying I could not comprehend it. Like Linji, I was struck hard and I didn't push back. Down to my toes, I did not know or understand. I went into my fear and grief and into his pain too, not with the thought of changing it, but just to go into it honestly. And I found this indigestible pain to be also very liberating. No longer outside of things, I was buoyed up by the universe. I didn't know why he was dying, but I trusted his dying. Now that I have lost him he is everywhere and also in me. I am my father now.

When we meet a new and difficult event we usually flee it or try to harmonize with it. What cannot be escaped or aligned with is awkwardness: the sacred grotesquerie in every relationship, whether with a tree, a job, or a person. When we embrace or enter that painful dissonance in our experience, we have the peace of someone who is in the right place in life. Even if we have just been struck or have been thrown in prison we will not suffer more than is right, because we are at peace with eternity. Awkwardness is so true that it pulls us to it, drawing us into the community of the real.

Snake Soup, a Madeleine, Winter Rain

When we are immersed in the great uncertainty and hardship, a companion and counter process arises, involuntary as a dream. A shard of the world appears, a consoling fragment, an awkward piece to save us. We notice something, we remember something, we are reminded of something—and this insignificant particle brings us out of the fog and into common life again. Resting in uncertainty and ambiguity, we have found a stillness, a space between things. Then the stillness itself throws up something new, like tulips out of the dark ground.

At such a moment, everything is particular with wonder. We don't distinguish between our pains and our pleasures. Pain can be transforming and liberating, pleasure can be sterile. We are fascinated with what is emerging before we are interested in its name. The Bodhisattva makes light by working close to the dark, by immersion in not-knowing. She lies down, like the dead god, in mystery. There, in what John of the Cross called "the lucky dark," glimpses and tastes appear. These will endure lifelong—summer lightning; a red fire engine in a sandbox; a walk on a beach during which a friend discussed suicide; a man with his head in his hands, weeping; hands that tremble and set the legs to tremble too; fingers enormous and the buttons they fumble with so small, so small; the body appearing for the first time, as amazing as the moon. We stumble upon these marvelous bits, bright not because of their content, but because they stand against the dark eternal ground. And the new life brings a sense of humor as well as wonder, the instinct of the moment as well as the ability to include the awkward, as an old Chinese story shows:

The temple cook was in a hurry and gathered a snake with the greens for the soup. Every one of these hungry vegetarians agreed the soup was delicious. Unfortunately, the Abbot found the head of the snake in his bowl. The cook was summoned. "Do you see this?" asked the Abbot. Immediately the cook seized the snake's head and ate it. "Oh, thank you," he said, and turning on his heel, he left.

Imagination first appears as redemption, the leap that saves us in an impossible moment. Later we realize that imagination is everywhere—the world dreaming us while we dream the world. But first, redemption. New life redeems the brokenness that went into its making. Infinitely divisible, life makes more life. Each piece is the child Horus being born, the infant Jesus waving his arms amid the straw in the manger.

Fragments are also secrets, treasures changed a little by their time in the dark cave. They can't quite be brought into the light, because they do not mean something, they *are*—life, the pieces in the shrine, endlessly assembled in endless ways. Repetition, a kiss, a way of caressing that developed because of not having a bed and embracing awkwardly in botanical gardens and cars, a part of the body that becomes an icon, the parts of the body—the upper arm, the curve of the belly—that become charged because they are near the hidden parts: all these fragments link us in the nets of life. We are all in pieces and all blessed.

Dreams, which are the soul's nightly accounting with itself, often display the condition of not-knowing and the new birth that follows. Here is the dream of a Buddhist teacher a little before he began to teach, a dream that shows disintegration as the beginning of independence and force.

> I was an unborn fawn in the belly of the doe. Coyotes began to chase the deer and I felt the rocking as the mother ran. Other deer escaped but the pregnant doe was not so fast and, though she fought hard, was pulled down and torn to pieces. I too was eaten. Only our bones were left, white bones on the stony ground. Then my bones reassembled and I leapt up. A

fierce strength came over me. I was exhilarated. "Watch out, coyotes," I yelled as I dashed toward them. The coyotes began to flee.

The person torn to pieces, eaten by life, and reassembled is a common shamanic theme. This dream allows us to understand the personal process underneath the mythic story of the god who dies and is reborn. There is wounding, mortification, loss. But something follows. Bones do not easily rot. Beyond birth and death, they are the life that is not destroyed even when we die. Since the dreamer here is still bones, we can also expect some further development as the soul inhabits the man more fully. The shaman, like the Bodhisattva, brings back knowledge for the benefit of the community, and this is the soul's goal as well, to bring the light of the spirit down to earth. Fragmentation doesn't mean only physical pain. It also refers to helplessness, the incompetence and clumsiness that seem such a part of being human, the Bodhisattva road. If we never know that helplessness, we have not engaged with this one, actual life.

The same teacher spoke of the way certain experiences restore him in difficult times.

I have wandered a lot, but I am always at home when I hear the sound of winter rain on the roof. It brings with it the wind, the gas fire, the smell of wet wool steaming. In my childhood, gales shook the house and my mother had us pray for the mariners. The fire and the weather bring back my grandfather. He would set his elbows on the blue Formica kitchen table, smoke Players cork-tipped cigarettes with an anchor on the package, and begin to talk. His stories led me out from my seat by the gas fire into Atlantic storms, dismastings, the eating of ship's rats, and other joys. When I am in pain, certain things just appear—memories, or tastes which bring memories, like sweet tea with milk. They make the world possible again.

Any bit of the universe can serve to restore the lot—each common piece having the power to make the world anew. For Proust, the taste of the madeleine soaked in tea was a door into childhood's garden, where the past was intact with its food, conversation, servants, grandmothers, and embraces. And through the past, the present became alive.

The pieces of the world are precisely so. For this man, it had to be the scent of damp wool, the sound of a winter gale; another scent, another noise, another taste wouldn't do. Long ago, Ling-yun was enlightened as he turned a bend and saw peach blossoms across the valley. Their crimson shocked him into a new life. For him, apple blossoms would never do. The eternal consoles us through the local genius of place, and everything ordinary has its own spell. We endure because of this spell. It remakes us out of the vast night and scatters us generously into the world.

The Monk's Child

Resting in the source makes us open. What we do not know allows the Tao to work on its own. When we can exist in uncertainty and receive things in the fog they are so often wrapped in, they will eventually become clear of themselves.

Hakuin was a grand old Japanese master who revived the enlightenment school of Zen. In late life he taught lords and village fishing people and was said to be at home with each. A story about him when he was young shows that even then he knew how to let life make life clear. Now this particular tale took place more than two centuries ago in a feudal town, but it also occurs today.

At the time, Hakuin was in training, scraping his living begging in the streets, and meditating late into the night. A beautiful girl lived near by. Hakuin did not think this a part of his story, but he was wrong, for the young girl was pregnant, and although she tried to hide it, nature took its course.

When her parents found out, the girl was not in an enviable position. "Who is the father?" they asked, but she wanted to protect him, and did not answer. Eventually, with a mixture of cajoling and threat, they broke down her resistance to some degree and she said, "It was the monk down the road who made me like this."

So the parents, who were impulsive like their daughter, swept up the baby, and burst through the door of Hakuin's little hut. "Here," they shouted, "you can't get away with this! We've heard all about monks like you. It's your baby. *You* take care of it." "Is that so?" said Hakuin, and held out his arms.

He then had to go out and beg food for the baby. Nobody wanted to give anything to such a monk, whose morals must have been terrible because—well, use your eyes. "What's the use of spending money on this one?" they would say. Meanwhile he had to meditate and rock the baby, wash the baby, feed the baby. This was not the life he had anticipated when he became a monk.

As time went on the young girl felt worse and worse. She

missed her child. Then she took her parents aside and said, "Look, I'm sorry, but that monk didn't have anything to do with me. I was just covering up for the fisher boy next door."

Without further consideration, the parents came bursting through the door of Hakuin's little hut. "Terribly sorry," they cried out. "Dreadful mistake. It wasn't you after all. We'll take the baby back now."

"Is that so?" said Hakuin, surrendering the child.

This "Is that so?" mind has many names. It is called, for example, "the jewel mirror meditation," the mirror that perfectly reflects everything that arrives in it. If an emu comes, an emu is reflected with its scrawny neck; if a baby comes, a baby is reflected, with its unfocussed eyes, and we meet it purely. At age sixty, the old Chinese master Zhaozhou Congshen wanted to refine his understanding before he began teaching. So he went on a twenty-year pilgrimage to meet the wisest people of the day. He said, "If I meet a hundred-year-old man and I have something to teach him, I will teach him, if I meet a child of eight and he has something to teach me, I will learn from him."

Along with Hakuin's receptive clarity, there is another point to the story of the infant. Someone has to want the baby, to speak for the baby, to claim the infant little valued, the child Moses, the baby Jesus. How many babies are brought into the world just like this? By accepting it, Hakuin says, "This is my child," and blesses the small life that the world has cast into his arms.

The way microscopic creatures live in hot volcanic vents in deep trenches in the Pacific, or albatrosses cruise in the gales of the great southern ocean, the Bodhisattva lives where the universe is always coming into being. It is an unusual but fundamentally natural habitat. Hakuin had empathy for the urgent life surrounding him, and this empathy is what makes him still interesting to us. We hear his story and we try to understand who might act as he did, imagining ourselves into his deeds and words. He had charity toward dreams and transgressions, fidelity to whatever life brought before him—babies, work, reading, the griefs of war and the musings of peace. Feeling the lives of others as her own, the Bodhisattva steps free of her own shape and self and passes through nothingness into the life of the other. If saving beings is the task of the Bodhisattva, imagining them is her method.

Imagining Things

The world's vast imagination throws up rivers and pines, statues of beautiful men and women found among ruins, war, people drinking mango sodas under umbrellas, ancient cities with narrow alleys, washing stretched high up in the sunshine between the balconies, shell holes in white walls, eucalyptus trees lying down on their elbows among termite mounds, red kangaroos, mathematics, and the quest for spiritual understanding. The mystery underneath us dreams, imagines, makes—and, in our humble and turbulent fashion, so do we imitate and praise it. The ancient Greek source of the word for *poet* means "maker," and when John Dunbar grieved his friends he called the poem "Lament for the Makers." But the imagination of the mystery itself makes us all up—flowers, stories, and the tellers of stories.

It is not our own, the imagination, it just brings things into being about us the way a coral island appears in the South Pacific, with its stacked-up overhanging cloud, its palms dipping in the trade wind, and its surf beating on the outer reefs. We do not cause the imagination or deserve it, yet it is intrinsically part of us and sustains us every day. We use the world's riches in the humblest fashion—wearing clothes and walking in the sunlight—and in this way shape ourselves as well as the world. Imagination links us to our origins—it summons us from nowhere and returns us there when it is done. A brightness fell out of Heaven and we carry it everywhere in our breasts—each puddle holds the same moon, the Chinese poets said—each of us a vial of primal light. When we make, when we imagine, we serve that source, we connect spirit and soul.

The Birth in Darkness of the Imagination

The fundamental human imaginative act is to see the other, to guess what the other needs, to engage with the other, to *be* the other, and to make thereby our own selves. Through this empathy, our fear of deep night gives way to a chastened sadness, an understanding of the poignancy of our situation. Expression is all, and yet life flows through and falls from us like a dream. So underneath our fear is a companionable loneliness, a serene light. This light is humble; it doesn't attempt brilliance, and there is nothing grandiose or selfish about it. It is a steady glow, full of kindness.

When we completely inhabit our fear, it reveals itself as a tenderness toward life. Then it leads us to make images, stories, music.

Basho in his travels encountered an ancient battlefield, with over-grown mounds and rusted bits of equipment in the dirt:

> Summer grass.
> Dreams of the warriors
> under the hill.

Here the wanderer has a memory of those he never knew, and is lonely for them, and his loneliness then spreads out like a kind of light, the taste of mortality leading into a timeless world.

At each new step, the walls we have built fall down like Jericho's. We are as afraid of changing as of failing to change—our alteration asks that we let ourselves fall into the outstretched arms of the world, into a sleep of what we already know. We have to trust that we will be awakened at the right time.

Perhaps you remember the story of the old, grand meditation teacher who late in life was still eager to learn. His wife of many years died. He grieved and, as many people do, seemed to take on some of her qualities. His friends thought him more intimate, more interested in the sort of close connections she used to bring into his life. It was as if she were still walking with him, and her going into the darkness was a going inside him, her companion. Nevertheless it was a hard period. He knew he had finally turned the corner when he was given a dream—of little flats of plants in a nursery, growing well and almost ready to be planted out.

Time is in those green plants, time and more tasks to do. Their life is delicate, but then nothing is as forceful as new things. When we are at the growing tip of life, our dreams are full of babies, young animals, seedling plants. The new work, the new music, the new idea, the developing consciousness, is finding a way to get into the world. The image of the greenhouse is important, too. Life is not fostered only by good fortune and fine weather. Everything— grief, refuse, the nondescript black material—feeds our imagination. Loss can bring us to the nursery.

Tears and Pearls

Here is an artist's dream of the creative process itself, of the soul-making and the links to spirit that are born in the darkness. The cousin in the dream is someone the dreamer is close to—another version, perhaps, of herself.

> My cousin is near the shore in a little shack, cultivating pearls and mother-of-pearl. There are various shells in a big vat. I pick up a shell—it's not an oyster, but more like a chambered nautilus, and very, very soft. I almost squash it trying to pull the pearl out. I realize it's too small yet and return the shell to the vat. The shells are fed with an extract of ginger, a hot, dense black substance. My cousin has her shack right next to her husband's big business. Her shack is very ordinary and no one notices what is going on. It's very dark in the shack.

In this dream, the imagination works invisibly, with the dark in the dark, making beauty and images of the spirit. Pearls come from the irritation of the mollusc: our suffering is transformed into jewels. Pearls are also the sea's mysterious treasure, they seem to encourage us to look down into them, and to remember our own depths. They are associated with Cleopatra, the Egyptian queen who, in the works of Shakespeare and Tiepolo, wore them on her compelling skin and drank them dissolved in vinegar; they hold the allure of life and the tears of beauty's passing. Afterwards, not thinking of her dream, the artist bought some teardrop pearl earrings, and these tears are also part of her inner journey. When we weep, we are released, and the lovely tears we wear are not about anything, they are just the tears of the way, swimming with a cloudy light, that seems to come from far inside.

About a year after her dream of growing pearls, the dreamer was in the country when the power went off during a storm. She was terrified. She remembered the suffocating closeness of air-raid shelters in Tokyo long ago, the sirens and the shocks of the bombing. Still, she made a decision unique for her: to go *with* the fear, to allow herself to be terrified, and with this acceptance came a flooding relaxation, a serenity and ease.

> I used to feel anxious and fill myself up with unnecessary things so that I didn't have to feel the fear. This time I stayed afraid. It was dizzying. Rather than blaming anyone for my state, I was just frightened. I thought, "I am just frightened. How extraordinary!" Being present is like standing on a cliff—exhilarating! I am getting softer on the outside and stronger on the inside.

Now the black ginger extract of the dream is starting to feed her in the day world. When this happens, when we do not turn away from our failures and insufficiencies, then what was dark becomes bright, what was painful becomes the occasion of release. In even the narrowest circumstances, life is a plenitude. To welcome life instead of fighting it, to befriend the moments of night, is to respect our embodiment and fulfill its tasks. We are simple then, happy or afraid or peaceful, and through that simplicity and openness, we are linked with each other. Meeting each other is possible.

Happiness Rises Out of the Ground

Happiness means resting in the light, not to get in the way, not to obscure what is naturally pouring forth. Insofar as there is any inside or outside, happiness comes from within. We just live in harmony with the currents of the wind, like the wavering lines of geese in the autumn sky, like the thick bull kelp undulating in the surf. As we continue on the journey without end, we no longer hold on to the light—the light adheres to us, in our weariness as well as in our joy. Where the primal stuff seemed dark, now, when we are happy, close to the earth, it seems bright even when it is dark. Doing nothing, we work through joy, feeling there is no separation between ourselves and what we are doing. Whatever rises before us is the answer we have always waited for, the thing for which we are grateful. It comes to us from before the beginning of time.

Consciousness is both our uniqueness and our adventure. Through it, we reflect and imagine. We see the snow, the stars, and the rain, the first plum blossoms thrust out in a pink haze, the girl crying in the wet street, and we see that each thing and being demonstrates its own portion of eternity.

This seeing blesses our lives—they are like us, these other inhabitants of earth, women and men, pigmented and pale, wolves and redwoods, brief beings hurtling into the dark; we share with them a mysterious nature. Each thing appears before us in its solitary radiance. What seemed solid before, now does not, and what seemed doomed seems now no longer fated to disappear.

The consoling and alarming discovery is that we are not bounded by our skin. What we witness, we become; we are not separate any more than we are lonely. We *are* the snow making a silence as it falls, the girl picking up her bicycle, the blossom adrift on the bough. This is the insight of Buddhism—an image of the jewelled net that holds the world and all of us in a seamless continuity. It is also the insight of creative process, the alchemy by which the harshest touch, the bitterest grief, is altered through our careful openness—an attention so persevering it becomes a kind of love—into something astonishing: a pain filled with immortal brightness. Refusing nothing of life, our sorrows, like pails of water, carry their gleam; our happiness suffuses the shadows as well as the light. In our transforming openness, we have been drinking what is simple, and it has made us drunk.

At Home with Han Shan

Long ago there was a Chinese sage called Han Shan. He abandoned his career and went to live on a mountain. When he shut the gate of his hermitage, he never expected to open it again. Released from his time, he became unattached, spontaneous, at ease with the pine scent and endless views that composed his life, and his poems have the pristine quality of the inner and outer wilderness.

Each age has its own tasks. For most of us now, our monasteries have no walls except the silence our meditation gathers to the center of our lives, and this is enough—it is more than enough. Our hermitage is the act of living with attention in the midst of things: amid the rhythms of work and love, the bath with the child, the endlessly growing paperwork, the ever-present likelihood of war, the necessity for taking action to help the world. For us, a good spiritual life is permeable and robust. It faces things squarely, knowing the smallest moments are all we have, and that even the smallest moment is full of happiness.

The young girl asks her father to call out words so that she can spell them. But in order to spell correctly, in order to concentrate perfectly, she must sing the letters—w-o-u-l-d, t-h-o-u-g-h-t, a-n-i-m-a-l—while skipping up and down the length of the kitchen, waving one hand and holding a bagel in the other. Thus she achieves perfect not-doing. It enables her to spell, to enter the community of readers and grown-ups.

The Bodhisattva harmonizes with uncertainty, with the dreaming power of the imagination, with the truth that the world beyond this one, toward which we yearn—the world we came from when we were born and that we half remember in lovely things; the world in which we are at home always, walking with our companions through swathes of sunlight and rainlight—is this very world. *This* kitchen with the water lilies painted on the floor by an artist friend, *this* sleepy child doing homework at the breakfast table. The life we yearn for is our own walking through common days; it is the ascent and the fall, the plateaus and recurrences, the moment of awakening and the moment of falling asleep. What we need, and what we love, what consoles us and what redeems us is here each moment, already within us. It waits for us to recognize its presence. We have only to give ourselves up to it, and our one life, and all life, welcomes us into its arms.

Notes

Some references were lost when I moved during the writing of this book. Where I have been unable to locate the source of a quotation I will be happy to give the attribution in future editions. The author will give gratitude and a small prize to the first people to correct a reference. Translation is also a problem. Some well-known Chinese and Japanese lines exist in many versions. I may think a version is my own when it is an unconscious memory of a previous translator. Again I will be happy to correct any errors.

CHAPTER 1. INVITATION TO THE JOURNEY
Issa's torn paper screen: This translation is by Michael Sierchio and
myself.

CHAPTER 2. THE WILDNESS INSIDE AND THE CREATURES TO
BE FOUND THERE
The story of Mr. Bugatti appeared in a book on racing cars I won as a
school prize long ago.

Rilke's "Archaic Torso of Apollo" in *The Selected Poetry of Rainer Maria Rilke,* ed. and trans. Stephen Mitchell (New York: Random House, 1982).

CHAPTER 3. DESCENT INTO NIGHT

Dante. This is a much-translated verse. As far as I know this is my version.

Innocence, the unexpected: *The I Ching or Book of Changes,* trans. R. Wilhelm and C. F. Baynes, Bollingen series XIX, ed. 3 (Princeton, N. J.: Princeton University Press, 1967). This quotation is from the commentaries in Part III, p. 510.

Rilke. How dear you will be to me then, you nights. *The Selected Poetry of Rainer Maria Rilke,* ed. and trans. Stephen Mitchell (New York: Random House, 1982).

T. S. Eliot. *Four Quartets* (New York: Harcourt Brace, 1971).

Kierkegaard on unconscious despair. In *The Sickness unto Death,* trans. Walter Lowrie in *Fear and Trembling* and *The Sickness unto Death* (Garden City, New York: Doubleday Anchor, 1954) p. 178.

CHAPTER 4. LOVE IN THE DARK TIME

Boland. If I defer the grief: From "The Pomegranate," in *In a Time of Violence* (New York: W.W. Norton, 1994).

Yeats: the foul rag-and-bone shop of the heart: From "The Circus Animals' Desertion." *The Collected Poems of W. B. Yeats* (New York: Macmillan, 1956).

Gary Snyder's rock: From "Paiute Creek." *No Nature: New and Selected Poems* (New York: Pantheon, 1992).

Coleridge. Blessing the water creatures: *The Poems of Samuel Taylor Coleridge* (London: Humphrey Milford Oxford University Press, 1935).

CHAPTER 5. CLIMBING INTO THE LIGHT

Wumen. It is imperative to cut off the mind road: From *The Gateless Barrier,* trans. Robert Aitken (Berkeley, Calif.: North Point Press, 1991), Case 1.

The fault, dear Brutus: Cassius's line about the stars is from Shakespeare's *Julius Caesar,* 1.2.139–40.

Stevens. not to think / of any misery: From "The Snow Man," in *The Collected Poems of Wallace Stevens* (New York: Alfred A. Knopf, 1954).

Walt Whitman, from "Song of Myself," 32, in *Leaves of Grass and Selected Prose* (New York: The Modern Library, 1950).

Ibsen fighting the trolls. A slightly different version of this famous saying appears in the notes to *Peer Gynt* trans. Rolf Fjelde (Minneapolis: University of Minnesota Press, 2nd ed. 1980), p. 222.

CHAPTER 6. THE FIRST SILENCE IN THE WORLD

Wumen Huaikai. Spring comes with its flowers: See *The Gateless Barrier,* in which Robert Aitken's translation is very near to this one.

Yeats. Fastened to a dying animal: From "Sailing to Byzantium" in *The Collected Poems of W. B. Yeats.*

Blake: From "Auguries of Innocence," in *The Complete Poetry and Prose of William Blake.* ed. David Erdman (Berkeley and Los Angeles: University of California Press, 1982).

Pascal: Noelle Oxenhandler in "Pascal's Jacket" *Parabola,* Fall 1994.

Stevens: From "The Snow Man," in *Collected Poems.*

Dōgen. Body and mind fallen away: From *Denkoroku: The Transmission of the Light,* trans. Robert Aitken (privately circulated).

Wordsworth: From "Composed upon Westminster Bridge, September 3, 1802" in *Selected Poems and Prefaces,* ed. Jack Stillinger (Boston: Houghton Mifflin, 1965).

In a well that has not been dug. This old Chinese poem appears with no author attribution in *Miscellaneous Koans*, a privately circulated Zen manuscript.

CHAPTER 7. THE ENLIGHTENMENT OF RIVERS AND GRASS

Wumen. Within nothingness, there is a road: From *The Gateless Barrier.*

I am pecking from inside: From The *Blue Cliff Record*. Trans. Robert Aitken (unpublished), Case 16.

Yuanwu's serving girl: Some of this story is in *Zen Letters: Teachings of Yuanwu*, trans. J. C. Cleary and Thomas Cleary (Boston: Shambala, 1994).

Changqing Da'an's white ox. This version is modified from I. Miura and R. F. Sasaki, *Zen Dust: The History of the Koan and Koan Study in Rinzai (Lin-Chi) Zen* (New York: Harcourt Brace & World, 1966, p. 74). Another version is in *The Transmission of the Lamp: Early Masters,* Comp. Tao Yuan, a Ch'an monk of the Sung Dynasty, trans. S. Ogata (Wolfeboro, N. H.: Longwood Academic, 1990), pp. 315–16.

Lingyun and the peach blossoms: A favorite Tong dynasty story. A version of his enlightenment verse is in *Zen Dust,* p. 292.

Keizan Jokin's village peach trees: From *Denkoroku: The Transmission of the Light,* trans. Robert Aitken, Case 13.

Yasutani. Robert Aitken tells this story.

Pang and Lingzhao fall down: R. F. Sasaki, *The Recorded Sayings of Layman P'ang* (New York: Weatherhill, 1971).

Dōgen: When the ten thousand things advance and confirm the self. Trans. Robert Aitken (unpublished).

CHAPTER 8. MORTIFICATION: THE SECOND DESCENT

Yangshan Huiji. Officially, even a needle cannot enter: This is my version.

Hakuin: P. B. Yampolski, *The Zen Master Hakuin* (New York: Columbia University Press, 1971). These are letters by Hakuin to students. The relevant letter is called "Orategama III," pp. 119–20.

Keats: Letter to George and Georgiana Keats, 21 April 1819.

Success is as dangerous as failure. *Tao te ching*, trans. Stephen Mitchell (New York: Harper & Row, 1988), Verse 13.

William Shakespeare. The uses of adversity. *As You Like It,* II, 1, l. 12.

William Shakespeare. Full fathom five. *The Tempest,* I, 2, l. 394.

William Shakespeare. *Othello,* 1.3 l. 169–171.

Repentance begs for burdens. Michel de Montaigne, *The Complete Essays,* trans. M. A. Screech. (London: Allen Lane / The Penguin Press, 1991) p. 29.

The Tao that can be named is not the eternal Tao. Lao Tse. Again there are many versions of this famous line. This is mine, probably borrowed from several sources.

Paul Tillich's dying day. René Tillich told me this story.

Confucius and the stolen sheep: Jonathan Spence in "What Confucius Said: Review of *The Analects of Confucius,*" trans. and notes by Simon Leys (Norton) *New York Review of Books,* Vol 44 #6 (April 10, 1997).

CHAPTER 9. CHARACTER AND INTEGRITY

John Beebe has developed an integration of Eastern and Western ideas of integrity. John Beebe, *Integrity in Depth*, College Station: Texas A&M University Press, 1992. The eastern theme of integrity seems to have begun with Lao Tse.

Jingqing. Trans. Robert Aitken (Unpublished).

Gauguin's questions. Robert Aitken related these to Zen and uses them in his teaching.

William Blake. If the fool would persist in his folly. From *The Marriage of Heaven and Hell. The Complete Poetry and Prose of William Blake,* ed. David Erdman. Berkeley and Los Angeles: University of California Press, 1982.

Shunryu Suzuki. By the earth we fall down, by the earth we stand up. Unpublished manuscript.

Obstruction. *I Ching,* trans. Wilhelm/Baynes, p. 152

Verba Seniorum, trans. Robert Walker. *Empty Sky* newsletter, Amarillo, Texas, March 1997.

Jumping off the cliff. Wumen Huaikai. There is a similar translation in *The Gateless Barrier,* Case 32.

The best way to combat evil is not directly but to make active progress for the good. *I Ching,* trans. Wilhelm/Baynes.

CHAPTER 10. GIFTS FROM THE SOURCE

Jianzhi Sengcan. Not picking and choosing: There are many slightly different translations of these famous lines. I haven't been able to find a source for this version; I think it belongs to Anonymous.

Issa. Don't worry, spiders, ed. Robert Hass, *The Essential Haiku. Versions of Basho, Buson, & Issa* (Hopewell, N.J.: Ecco Press, 1994).

Keizan Jokin. Hazy moon on a spring night. *Transmission of the light,* Case 7. The translations are slight variants of those by Robert Aitken which are privately circulated for Zen students. A good version of the source text is *The Record of Transmitting the Light: Zen Master Keizan's Denkoroku,* trans. Frances H. Cook (Los Angeles: Center Publications, 1991).

John Keats on negative capability: A letter to George and Thomas
Keats, dated probably 21 or 27 December 1817, Hampstead. In
Selected Poems and Letters. Ed. with introduction and notes by
Douglas Bush. Cambridge, Mass.: The Riverside Press, 1959.

Bodhidharma and Emperor Wu. This is more or less Robert Aitken's
unpublished translation.

Linji. This is my version of an old story that appears in *The Zen
Teachings of Master Lin-Chi*, trans. Burton Watson (Boston and
London: Shambhala, 1993).

St John of the Cross. The lucky dark. *Poems of St John of the Cross*,
trans. John F. Nims (Chicago: University of Chicago Press, 1979).

Snake soup. This is my version of a story that also appears, told by
Nyogen Senzaki, in *Zen Flesh, Zen Bones: A Collection of Zen
and Pre-Zen Writings*, comp. Paul Reps (Rutland, Vt.: Tuttle,
1957).

The monk's child. This is my telling of another of Nyogen Senzaki's
stories in *Zen Flesh, Zen Bones*.

Zhaozhou Congshen's pilgrimage. The story is told in *Radical Zen.
The Sayings of Joshu*, trans. Yoel Hoffman (Brookline, Mass.:
Autumn Press, 1978).

Basho: Summer grass. My translation.

Contacts for Comments or Queries

California Diamond Sangha

www.ca-diamond-sangha.org

P. O. Box 2972
Santa Rosa, California   95405
USA
707 793 2138
510 531 5779

John Tarrant

johnt@wco.com

P.O. Box 2346
Santa Rosa, California   95405